THE COUNTRYSIDE WE WANT

The Countryside We Want

A Manifesto for the Year 2000

Edited by **CHARLIE PYE-SMITH** and **CHRIS HALL**
Photographs by **FAY GODWIN**

GREEN BOOKS

First published by
Green Books
Hartland
Bideford
Devon, EX39 6EE

Cover: Simon Willby

British Library Cataloguing in Publication Data
The countryside we want : a manifesto for the year 2000
1. Nature conservation—Great Britain
2. Landscape conservation—Great Britain
I. Pye-Smith, Charlie
333.76'16'0941   QH77.G7

ISBN 1 870098 04 8

Typeset by KMA Typesetting
70 The Square, Hartland, Devon

Printed by Robert Hartnoll (1985) Ltd.
Victoria Square, Bodmin, Cornwall

The Countryside We Want is printed on 100% recycled paper

Contents

THE 1999 COMMITTEE

Chair: Peter Melchett

The 1999 Committee was an informal group brought together by Peter Melchett in Autumn 1984. The sole purpose of the Committee was to produce this book, and regular meetings were held during 1985 and 1986. We would like to thank the World Wildlife Fund, UK for generously supporting some of the research for this book. The views expressed are those of the committee members, and do not necessarily represent those of WWF UK.

Stephen R. L. Clark is Professor of Philosophy at Liverpool University.

Brian Duffield is Director of the Scottish Centre for Physical Education, Movement and Leisure Studies, Moray House College of Education, Edinburgh.

Chris Hall is Chairman of the Ramblers' Association

Peter Melchett is a farmer in Norfolk who is involved in a number of conservation and amenity organisations.

Chris Rose works for World Wildlife Fund International.

Robbie Stoakes is Director of Leisure Services for the London Borough of Hounslow.

Andrew Warren lectures in Geography and Conservation at University College, London.

Bryn Green, Howard Newby and Richard Mabey also joined in the discussions.

The Countryside We Want was edited by Charlie Pye-Smith and Chris Hall.

Foreword

THIS BOOK was written at a time of great confusion about the future of the British countryside. The agricultural orthodoxy of nearly half a century—that our countryside exists to produce more and yet more food at any price—is finally being overturned. But in its place arise new demons: hideous blocks of conifers threaten to blanket valleys as well as hills, and great dollops of expensive housing may come to obliterate green belts and open countryside. Farmers, nature conservationists, walkers and rural workers are fighting desperate and rearguard actions against these and other evils. We need a new vision of what our countryside should be and a manifesto to achieve it. That is what this book provides.

We make no claim to have produced a set of entirely new ideas. But we do believe that the bringing together of these ideas is new. We have tried to rethink a series of hitherto separate policies for rural areas and to weld them into a coherent whole which, if adopted, would guarantee a truly beautiful, varied, productive and peaceful countryside. The protagonists of the policies we endorse have often deliberately pursued them in isolation from each other. People concerned about nature conservation have not considered the problems of animal welfare. Those who care about landscapes have ignored the social and economic difficulties of the places they want to conserve. Our aim has been to bridge these divides and to offer a comprehensive vision of the future; one that embraces social and economic issues, the enhancement and conservation of the environment and the welfare of wildlife and farm animals.

The members of The 1999 Committee, who came together to write this manifesto, represent a variety of interests, even though many of us would be considered 'environmentalists'. We came together deliberately to take a broader view, and to try and look at the countryside of the future with people concerned about social and economic issues, and the welfare of wild and farm animals. We may not share a single political ideology, but we have agreed on a coherent set of policies.

Inevitably, many people will be as enraged by the things we have omitted as by what we have included. The 1999 Committee contained no women, and many interests were not represented. Some may feel that we have failed to discuss some of the more serious threats to the countryside such as nuclear power, but we have tried to limit ourselves to the issues which are particular to rural areas. It is because of this that we have not tackled general questions of disarmament, although we acknowledge that a healthy and prosperous countryside cannot exist as long as the threat of nuclear annihilation remains with us. Indeed we haven't discussed in any detail the use and abuse of the countryside for military training purposes. The peace and tranquillity of the countryside are frequently shattered by military manoeuvres of one sort or another. Walk along the beautiful coast of Dorset, and you have to struggle on permitted days through the military firing-range of Lulworth. Go for a family holiday in the Lake District, and have the peace of the countryside and your peace of mind shattered by low-flying military jets. From the Dartmoor National Park in the west and the Norfolk brecklands in the east to the Northumberland National Park in the north, the military seems to be everywhere in our countryside, and its presence excludes almost all of the interests we want to advance through the policies we set out in this book.

We must admit also to some geographical omissions. This book concerns itself with the countryside we want to see in Great Britain. We have excluded Northern Ireland completely, and we have largely omitted the detailed discussion that would be necessary to translate our ideas and objectives, and particularly the mechanisms for achieving these, into specific recommendations for Scotland. Once again, we had to impose some limits on ourselves if we were to go into enough detail to make our ideas credible—and keep this book a readable length. However, we have drawn on Scotland for examples of some of the things which are wrong with the British countryside; indeed it provides a depressingly rich source for this purpose. We believe that the ideas we put forward in this book are applicable to Scotland, with such changes as are necessary to take account of the structure of local government, and the differences in law and practice north of the border. While the priorities for change in Scotland may be different, and the mechanisms for achieving it will be different, we see no reason why our vision should not apply in the highlands and islands of Scotland just as it will in the uplands of England and Wales, and to the Scottish lowlands just as it will to lowland areas in the north of England.

While we apologise to anyone who is offended by these omissions, whether of geography or policy, we do not believe that they detract significantly from our overall aim. We believe we have produced a manifesto for the countryside that breaks new ground in bringing together a number of isolated interests to produce a coherent set of policies for the countryside of the future. We hope we have done this at a length and in a style that will appeal to specialists and non-specialists alike. One of our main aims has been to provide inspiration for conservationists, and a goal for them to work towards. We believe that all those concerned with nature and landscape conservation in this country have, for too long, been on the defensive. Their objectives have been to limit damage, to slow down the rate of destruction. This must change. We must not only stop the destruction of jobs, rural services, wildlife and landscape—we must implement policies that will lead to real improvements.

We hope that this manifesto will reach a wide audience. In particular, we want to influence those politicians who represent rural communities, and rural communities themselves. We believe that politicians of all parties have, at worst, neglected the particular problems of rural areas or, at best, seriously underestimated the scope and extent of the changes that are needed.

Anyone looking ahead more than a year or two, and certainly anyone looking ahead the twenty-odd years that we have taken as our time-scale, is bound to be wrong in some respects. Inevitably, we will be seen to have missed major changes which we ought to have foreseen and others which are unforeseeable. Nevertheless, we believe that profound changes must take place in the British countryside, and our purpose will be achieved if the ideas in this book become part of the conventional wisdom long before the turn of the century. Indeed, by then, we hope they will be seen as old hat.

Peter Melchett

Introduction

*T*HE COUNTRYSIDE WE WANT is a manifesto, not an idly contemplated utopia, unattainable in our lifetime or beyond. Utopias may have their uses, but we see no point in producing a plan whose idealism would mean that it gathered more dust than followers. At the same time we profoundly dislike wishy-washy, consensus-loving documents which attempt to reconcile conflicts between different groups of people by pretending they don't exist, or by suggesting that if we all sat round a table and talked sensibly the problems would go away. The British countryside is too important to us for that kind of fudging. *The Countryside We Want* is a practical programme of reforms for revitalising rural Britain and halting the many destructive processes which yearly make it a less attractive place to live in and visit.

We must begin by stating clearly the premises from which we have worked. We believe that no one group of individuals has any greater claim on the countryside than any other. We all have an interest in the land, the industrial labourer no less than the farmer. Individual freedom is one of the main considerations of political philosophy, and it can only exist if we all have the opportunity to participate in shaping the environment. Decisions, wherever possible, should be made not in some remote bureaucracy but by elected men and women in daily contact with their constituents. In outlook we are unashamedly decentralist. Freedom implies choice, and if we are to pay it anything more than lip service we must create a countryside in which the greatest number of opportunities exists for its use and enjoyment. We want a diverse countryside in which a multiplicity of activities can take place.

Recent shifts in government thinking, although pointing confusedly towards such an ideal, still fall far short of altering the long-standing emphasis on food and timber production.

We are concerned here with the countryside, but we recognise that the division between town and country is in many ways artificial. Town and country are no longer the separate entities which they once were, or seemed to be. Some people in the countryside still talk despairingly about 'townees', and some people in our towns still imagine that there are 'countryfolk' whose way of life, moral character and outlook are substantially different from theirs. This is all false. Town and country people watch the same television programmes, shop in the same places, do mostly the same jobs, live on similar estates—and derive the same kinds of pleasure and use from the countryside. The barriers which divide town from country are largely illusory, and the only people who profit from their continued recognition are the rural landowners who wish to protect their privileges and ensure that the urban majority has no say in what they are doing to 'their land'. Our intention is that it is not only those who live in the country who should decide the fate of the land but that townspeople should also make their choices.

The countryside will always be changing. By the end of this century we shall be farming in different ways, working with new technologies in new jobs, and demanding different things from the countryside. Even our perceptions of what is beautiful may have changed. Our task is not to create an idealised countryside, which, once created, must be frozen and protected from innovation, but to bring all the demands on the countryside into a state of harmony. However, there is not the slightest chance of achieving a healthy countryside if the prevalent utilitarian view, which holds that resources have no value unless they generate wealth, continues to be favoured by those in power. At present, work is only considered 'productive' if it creates a commodity which can be sold in the market-place (or, into intervention stores); and there is a tendency among politicians to sneer at jobs whose aim is to look after the countryside We must encourage an attitude which values the worker who looks after footpaths or manages woodlands as highly as the worker who produces potatoes or pigs. The benefits to society should not be measured solely in pecuniary terms. And in any case, many of the agricultural activities which are subsidised by government—by us, in other words—are in the worst interest of the countryside and the consumer, often channelling money from those who can't afford it to those who don't need it, and destroying what we cherish in order to produce more of what already exists in plenty.

The policies which determine the fate of Britain's countryside today are narrow in outlook and based on short-term expediency and greed. The Scott Committee, which was given the task of formulating future land-use policies during the Second World War by the government, suggested, not surprisingly in the circumstances, that self-sufficiency in food should become a primary objective of post-war agricultural policy. With one exception, the committee foresaw no conflict between agriculture and conservation; "a radical alteration of the types of farming is not probable and no striking change in the pattern of the countryside is to be expected". They were wrong. But what is remarkable is not that the committee failed to foresee the colossal destruction of wildlife and landscape which was to occur over the coming decades, but that future governments should persistently refuse to acknowledge that agricultural 'progress' was destroying the countryside when it was plain for all to see.

The major government reviews of the 1970s (*Food From Our Own Resources* and *Farming and the Nation*, for example) did little more than echo the Scott Report's preoccupation with producing more and more food. Any recognition in these documents that the countryside had functions unrelated to the production of food and timber was no more than platitudinous. The effects of new technologies on jobs and labour were ignored. Insidious social change, which was leaving a dwindling and poverty-stricken residue of indigenous country-dwellers marooned among a rising mass of affluent suburban exiles, went largely unremarked. And no thought was given to the ill effects which our own policies and methods of food production were having on many Third World countries. Since we joined the Common Market in 1973, the arguments urging further self-sufficiency in food production have been little more than elaborate sophistries, designed in the UK to keep the landed interests happy (and rich).

What has been lacking is a vision of what the countryside might become, not next year or the year after, but a generation hence. *The Countryside We Want* tries to provide such a vision. We are not concerned with the minutiae of policy, but with radical reforms which will create a countryside in which both human and wildlife will prosper. Where more people work on the land. Where everyone can wander freely. Where the animals which end up on our plates are decently kept and decently killed. And where methods of production make wise use of natural resources and place no unnecessary burden, financial or otherwise, on the inhabitants of this country or those of others.

CHAPTER ONE

You've Never Had It So Bad

You've Never Had It So Bad

IN THE British psyche the countryside is inextricably linked with notions of freedom. We see our cities and towns, with their abrupt and concrete horizons, as planned and artificially rigid. In contrast, the countryside—the place where one can 'get away from it all'—carries the seemingly anarchic stamp of raw and unpredictable nature. The naive idyll of happy, carefree rusticity dies hard; but a glance at the countryside today shows it never to have been more illusory.

Take, for example, your 'freedom to roam'. You hardly have any. Walking is the most popular active pastime in the British countryside yet the overwhelming bulk of the countryside is held and managed for agriculture or forestry without any provisions for public access. Even in the national parks, one of whose aims is to provide access 'for open air public enjoyment', the visitor is still barred from walking where he or she wishes. The presumption in law is that public access is the exception, not the rule. In the rich agricultural districts of southern England you can waste much time and petrol just looking for a public footpath, and there's a good chance that when you find one it will have been ploughed up or planted over.

Forty years ago, the British countryside was rich in wildlife, varied in landscape and colour, and more densely populated than it is today. But since the last war great chunks have been turned into corn prairies, and deciduous woodlands whose continued existence could be traced back to the Domesday Book of 1086 have been felled and replaced with rows of conifers whose silence, even in spring, indicates their sterility for wildlife. Over the last forty years between a third and a half of our ancient woodlands have been lost. Sixty per cent of our fens have been drained to make way for crops, many of which we now produce in surplus. And the heathlands which once spread across much of southern England have been reduced to tiny fragments.

Many species once common are now facing extinction. For example, between 1930 and 1980 the snake's head fritillary, a plant of damp meadows, had its range reduced from one hundred and sixteen sites to just seventeen. This was because its habitat had been 'improved' (the agricultural euphemism for destruction). The use of agricultural chemicals has also had severe effects on many species. In the late 1950s and early 1960s the peregrine falcon suffered a fifty per cent reduction in numbers. The decline was caused by persistent pesticides like DDT working their way up the food chain. Not long ago the otter could be found on virtually every British river. Its absence from most of the country today can be attributed to both habitat loss and pesticides.

While most of those animals and plants which are getting rarer are the victims of practices whose purpose is to produce more food and timber rather than to kill them, some species are shot, trapped, hunted and poisoned because they are seen as being in direct conflict with man. It seems to be an axiom of game 'management' that the natural predators of pheasant and grouse must be killed in order that another predator—man—can slaughter greater numbers of the prey, ritually, at a later date. Peregrine, buzzard, golden eagle and other hawks and owls are still shot and poisoned on gaming estates, even though they are protected by law. A gamekeeper's gibbet, still a common enough sight, provides an inventory of the other 'vermin' which are killed for the sake of the shoot: stoats, weasels, jays, magpies, crows, pigeons, rats, adders...

Leaving aside, for the moment, our right to kill (or, seen from the victim's point of view, the right not to be killed), this loss of wildlife represents diminishing choice for those who seek to enjoy the countryside. Thirty or forty years ago an inhabitant of London could choose, when taking a day out in the countryside, whether to walk through an oak forest, across a heath, beside a fen or over the rich sward of 'unimproved' chalk downland: all were within easy reach of the capital. That choice no longer exists. Modern farming and commercial forestry have pared these habitats away, and even if the visitor finds what he or she is looking for, it is likely to be poorer in sound, smell and looks than it once was. The chance of visitors finding such places or, having found them, being able to explore them for themselves, is also much reduced. Precisely because such sights and sounds have become rare, they are guarded and interpreted in ways which, however well meant, must diminish both physical freedom and the intellectual rewards of discovery.

Changes in farming practices have also made the farm itself a less diverse and interesting place. Intensification has driven animals like the pig and the hen off the farm and into huge factory units. Meanwhile, the financial incentives of the Ministry of Agriculture, Fisheries and Food (MAFF) and the EEC have encouraged farmers to specialise in arable crops. Many counties in the south and east have been given over almost entirely to growing cereals. The farms are often bereft of natural and semi-natural features—why bother keeping hedges when they take up valuable space?—and consequently devoid of wildlife. These are monochrome landscapes: green in spring, yellow in autumn and green or brown again in winter. Anything which doesn't give a direct financial return is seen as a weed or a pest. Over much of lowland Britain sprays are used to kill everything apart from the money-maker. A wheat field is exactly that—wheat: no hares, no corn-cockles, no poppies, no butterflies.

Visitors to the countryside have never had it so bad, and neither have farm animals, many of which must live out their lives in cruel confinement. The pig and the hen have suffered most. Ninety-six per cent of the eggs on the market come from battery hens, which are crammed four to a cage measuring sixteen inches by eighteen. The birds can neither fly, nor spread their wings, nor dust themselves—all activities which would be part of their daily routine were they outdoors. The battery hen-house has more in common with a medieval lunatic asylum than a farm. Stress leads to aggression and abnormal behaviour; cannibalism is by no means rare. Broiler birds and turkeys are also reared under intensive conditions. The aim is to get as much meat as possible, as fast as possible, using the least possible amount of energy (in the form of feed).

The outdoor pig herd is not quite a thing of the past, but two-thirds of our breeding sows now spend their lives in what amounts to solitary confinement. The sow passes her pregnancy in a dry sow-stall. She lies, virtually unable to move, on a concrete floor, her rear end stretched over slats which allow dung and urine to fall through. When she is due to farrow she is moved to a farrowing crate. Her litter is removed after three weeks. She is put to the boar again (often being lined up with other sows in a 'rape-rack'), then returned to a dry sow-stall. If her progeny are not to be used as breeding stock, they are fattened up for pork or bacon. The latest perversion consists of a battery pig system similar to that used for hens.

Cattle, too, are subjected to varying degrees of confinement. Many dairy herds are 'zero-grazed': grass is cut and taken indoors to them, rather than vice versa. More infamous is the system by which many veal calves are reared.

White veal comes from calves reared in twenty-four-inch pens. They are kept, throughout their brief lives, in semi-darkness, and they are fed an iron-deficient diet to induce anaemia. Admittedly, MAFF are now ending the worst abuses, and most of our veal calves are already reared in groups in straw yards—but we still import crated veal from continental countries, and many of these begin their lives in this country. Restaurant veal is almost invariably of the tortured variety.

For a farm animal, death may be a release from suffering; but it is often far from quick and painless. There is widespread abuse of animals in both markets and abattoirs. Over ten per cent of lambs are damaged badly enough in transit to reduce their value, and the figure for pigs is even higher. Animals are supposed to be unconscious when their throats are slit, but ineffective stunning systems and carelessness (or callousness) on the part of slaughter-gangs, who are paid headage rates, means that many animals face the knife fully conscious.

The British are becoming increasingly aware of what they eat. This is just as well, as many diseases which are common killers in the western world are related to poor diet. We eat too much fat, too much sugar, and not enough vegetables or fibre. Astonishingly, agricultural policy has never taken account of the relationship between poor diet and ill health. Not only is the national diet unbalanced, much of the food we eat is contaminated by poisons from the farm. Ninety-nine per cent of our cereals and vegetables are sprayed with one or more pesticides between sowing and harvesting, and it is not uncommon for a wheat crop to receive ten or more different pesticides. There is no statutory system of controls to limit pesticide residue in food, but spot-checks have found traces of aldrin on mushrooms and DDT on blackcurrants and lettuce. The Royal Commission on Environmental Pollution considered that DDT was so dangerous that its use should be banned. That was in 1970.

Since then horticulturists have continued their use of DDT, and it is one of several dangerous chemicals which find their way into our stomachs. The EEC has introduced two directives which fix mandatory limits for some pesticide residues, but the UK has insisted that these limits should not have to be imposed in the UK before 1991.

In this country we do not have a statutory system of labelling to tell us where what we buy came from and how it was treated. A piece of beef may come from a suckler-herd reared on unsprayed and unfertilised upland pastures. Or (more probably) it may come from intensively reared cattle, raised indoors and fed on concentrates. The food industry is opposed to honest and informative labelling. The reason for this is very simple: if we were given a choice we might exercise it in favour of those maverick farmers who produce food by means of which we approve. If we were allowed to vote with our mouths, the high-tech, intensive systems of production would be faced by a diminishing demand for their produce.

What about the people who work the land? At the end of the last war there were one million farm workers in Britain. Less than a third now remain. Throughout the 1970s the farm labour force declined at the rate of about four per cent a year; between 1960 and 1986 nearly half the jobs in agriculture and horticulture were lost. At the same time labour productivity rose by over six per cent a year. Fewer people are producing more and more food, and successive governments have not been slow to cite this as a vindication of their growth-obsessed agricultural policies. However, the human costs have been considerable. Recently the fastest growing category of worker has been the unemployed, in the country as in the cities. The decline of farm-labour has been particularly dramatic in the uplands. And today less than a sixth of those who live and work in the countryside are employed on farms. Those who do still work on farms are generally poorly paid. The basic working week (forty hours) is longer than in most industries and basic wages remain well below the industrial average. Even with long periods of overtime, many agricultural workers are eligible for Family Income Supplement.

Nor has it been only the workers who have suffered. Every year many small farmers go out of business. Between 1983/4 and 1984/5 the income of small dairy farmers fell from an average of £3,903 to £3,633, while that of large, specialist cereal farms rose from £39,205 to £48,256. Again, the hills have had the worst of it. Governments have responded to the plight of those who farm in the Less Favoured Areas (LFAs) with a complex system of subsidies. Incentives come in the form of headage payments,and these, together with other support devices, have undoubtedly encouraged production, but they have neither arrested depopulation nor saved the small and part-time farmer from bankruptcy. Indeed, the larger farmers have profited at the expense of the smaller ones. In a comprehensive survey in the early 1980s it was shown that the seven hundred and fifty nine largest farmers in the LFAs of England and Wales received average headage payments of over £13,000. The eleven thousand smallest farmers got less than £600 each. Since then some of the latter have gone out of business.

'Think big' has been the government's message to farmers and foresters. And many of those who have had the capital to expand, or whose assets enabled them to borrow heavily—agricultural indebtedness in early 1987 stood at a staggering £5,600 millions—have done so. The number of farms in England has been declining at two per cent a year. During the 1970s, eighty per cent of the land which came onto the market was bought by farmers expanding their holdings. In counties like Norfolk over half the farms are five hundred acres or more. Gradually, the smaller farms are being subsumed by the larger ones.

Rural Britain is now middle-class Britain. Over the past few decades the social composition of rural communities has been dramatically altered. Most of those who live in our villages work in nearby towns. Most villages are no longer agricultural communities, and social polarisation between an affluent majority and a relatively deprived and poor minority has become increasingly marked. We now find this majority, most of whom are recent arrivals, deciding quite democratically that services vital to the less well off, public transport being the most obvious example, should be cut in return for lower levels of taxation.

The picture, then, is one of a countryside which becomes daily less varied and interesting. Land has become an economic commodity to be worked as intensively as possible to produce more of what we often already have in surplus. Some changes in the countryside sprang from the new technologies which revolutionised agricultural practice since the last war. Horse-power gave way to the tractor, smaller machines to bigger ones. Pesticides enabled farmers to foresake crop rotation and grow the same crop on the same field year after year, and the use of artificial fertilisers, which has increased tenfold since 1950, has enabled lowland farmers to dispense with manuring stock and concentrate on cereals. However, it has been government policy which has been the real determinant of how farmers have changed their ways. For forty years the Ministry of Agriculture encouraged farmers to increase production regardless of the costs to wildlife, landscape and communities. The landowning minority's political clout has been enormous, and the Ministry of Agriculture has frequently behaved more like the lap-dog of the National Farmers' Union than an arm of democratically elected government, disposing of huge amounts of subsidy and cash to encourage those very activities which other government departments and agencies, charged with conserving the countryside, must strive to halt.

No government has ever tried to develop a fair way of controlling agricultural and forestry development. Private interests are simply left to do what they want, regardless of the consequences for the public interest. The Nature Conservancy Council (NCC) and the Countryside Commissions have proved no match for MAFF and the Forestry Commission. As though in recognition of this, the NCC has received a consolation prize in the shape of limited and temporary delaying powers. (Farmers must notify the NCC of their intentions to 'develop' land designated as a 'Site of Special Scientific Interest'.) Admittedly, we do have nature reserves. And some of our rarer plants and animals are protected by law. But the vast bulk of the countryside is neither owned nor controlled by conservation bodies, and farmers and foresters can do pretty much as they please with it. The 1981 Wildlife and Countryside Act has proved inadequate. Many claimed, with good reason, that it was little more than a get-well card from Parliament to an ailing countryside. It failed to provide the means to halt further destruction of woods and fens, heaths and moorlands. The suggestion that landowners and land-managers should be subject to public controls over what they do to the land produces the retort that this would be a denial of freedom. But what and whose freedom?

There is a fine old democratic principle that one should grant 'the maximum liberty compatible with an equal liberty for all'. This may be an impracticable ideal, but it is a sensible guide to reform. Following it, we would come nearer to an equitably run countryside. For the freedom on which the countryside's present owners and managers insist is the freedom to deny us access to the land, to deprive us of the rich and variegated landscape we once enjoyed, to rear animals in conditions many of us find abhorrent, to douse the fields with chemicals that kill wildlife and pollute drinking-water. These are not freedoms we feel called upon to respect.

CHAPTER TWO

Mores and Morals

Mores and Morals

SYMPTOMATIC of our age are utilitarian values, and conservationists have been wary of expressing the moral, romantic and aesthetic reasons why they wish to conserve nature. Such timidity, as we shall argue shortly, is stupid. When opposing a development at a public inquiry, conservationists will often put forward an economic argument against the developer, assuming they can find one. Such an argument is not so much an argument for conservation as one against development. In a society where the gods of profit and materialism have won the minds of so many whose responsibility it is to allocate natural resources, a heavy reliance on economic arguments is perhaps inevitable. Decision-makers, with a few eccentric exceptions, prefer to save money, or help others to make it, rather than spend it.

Not that economic arguments are bad ones; they are just limited. At times they have undoubtedly helped the cause of conservation. For example, conservationists have managed to show that MAFF has consistently used spurious cost-benefit analyses to justify the drainage of wet meadows and the reclamation of salt marshes. At a public inquiry investigating whether a water authority should drain the wet pastures of Amberley Wildbrooks in Sussex it was the economic argument which persuaded the inspector against the authority. Economic arguments in favour of bringing more marginal land into intensive food-production have now been discredited, and MAFF has been forced to reduce grant-aid for activities such as land-drainage (though rather too late, sadly, to save most wetlands).

The scientific criterion is as likely to be abused at public inquiries as the economic. The claim that ecologists could make real contributions to land-use decision-making drew authenticity from the two post-war touchstones of planning and science, and the Nature Conservancy Council (NCC), which was established in 1949, became the institutional apotheosis of scientific conservation. One of its duties is to identify the country's most important wildlife sites, which, tellingly, are known as 'Sites of Special Scientific Interest' (SSSIs). It is a moot point whether scientific arguments have been effective in safeguarding nature.

For many people the driving motive in conservation is anxiety about the future, and anxiety springs from a mismatch between an ideal and a prediction. Our ideals are fashioned out of a complex mix of emotion and desire, morals and ideology. Prediction, on the other hand, relies, or should rely, on scientific facts. But mortal man, however well-intentioned, can never hope to make long-term predictions which are wholly reliable, about, say, the effects that a certain development will have on a certain species. Evidence for this abounds.

In some cases conservationists have been downright mischievous, dressing their predictions in pseudo-science to give respectability to anxieties which were largely emotional in origin and self-interested in purpose. A classic example of bogus science being used to validate environmental anxiety comes from America. Hugh Hammond Bennett, the founder of the US Soil Conservation Unit, studied soil erosion during the 1930s. He used a minimum of facts to generate great gloom about soil losses on croplands. The time was certainly ripe: the nation had been softened up by Steinbeck's *The Grapes of Wrath*, which vividly portrayed the human tragedies of dust-bowl farming. Bennett organised the maps of erosion, which, if believed, would have consigned the states of Missouri, Kansas, and Iowa to long-term sterility. These three states are now major contributors to America's huge grain surplus.

None of this is to say that science cannot and has not played a part in helping conservationists achieve their ends. The chemist is crucial to the study of water pollution; the microbiologist helps us understand how diseases spread, and therefore how they can be combated; and the ecologist has shown how and why animal populations fluctuate. Scientific studies should also help to dispel the myths which have led to the persecution of certain species. Fox-hunters want us to believe that foxes are devious, cruel, cunning and vicious killers; and farmers maintain that foxes kill their lambs. However, a recent study carried out by MAFF found that foxes accounted for only one half a per cent of lamb losses in a Welsh study-area, and when scientists compared lamb mortality rates in two areas of Scotland—one with foxes and one without—they found them identical. Scientific study has helped to show that, contrary to what most farmers and all fox-hunters think, foxes seldom cause problems for the farmers.

In short, science's contribution to conservation has been mixed. By laying so much stress on 'scientific importance', conservationists have underplayed the moral issues involved. And scientists have frequently expended much energy on futile research projects (one thinks, for example, of the work investigating the effects of trampling on upland vegetation), while ignoring issues of much greater importance. Not nearly enough work has been done on problems such as acid-rain damage to flora and fauna or the dumping of radioactive waste at sea. And although environmental scientists have researched the toxic effects of chemicals like DDT, hardly any work has been done on the effects which apparently less persistent pesticides have on the environment—the Game Conservancy is the only organisation that has been studying the effects of these on cereal ecosystems.

The idea that economic and scientific arguments carry more force than those which hinge on moral or romantic perceptions does not bear examination. Frequently we can make out a case for conservation which is couched in terms of economic prudence. But to say that we wish to conserve Welsh hay-meadows or Kentish chalk grassland or Norfolk marshes only because it makes economic sense would be untrue. Our real motivation transcends the mundane business of using resources in a sustainable way or saving animals and plants from extinction.

The whole identity of the British people is linked inextricably with the countryside. Less than two centuries ago over half the population made its daily living in the fields, and although the number of farm workers has dwindled to less than two hundred thousand, the landscape, despite the ravages of the last forty years, still provides a chronicle of past achievements and struggles. The hedgerows whose destruction we mourn today are a reminder of the enclosure acts, which were used to dispossess the peasantry of their common lands. The dykes which criss-cross the Fens tell us of the farmers' constant struggle against encroaching waters. The grassed-over spoil heaps in the Pennine dales revive memories of the nineteenth-century lead-mines.

In our literature, music, painting and architecture, the countryside has always been a primary inspiration. It has been not only the obvious nature writers—for example, John Clare, Richard Jefferies or Edward Thomas—who have drawn their themes from our fields and mountains. As H.J. Massingham wrote of Shakespeare, "He made use of natural symbols for atmospheric, emotional, and dramatic purposes, and grouped them together to form a power-station for each play... Natural imagery in Shakespeare is thus woven into the very fabric of his art." Milton, Keats, Shelley, Charlotte Brontë and many others owed just as much to the countryside. And one only has to look at today's advertisements and television programmes to see that rural beauty still exercises great influence. The posters welcoming visitors to Britain depict idyllic country scenes. Chocolate boxes are covered with glossy reproductions of *The Hay Wain* and programmes like the Herriot vet series have an enduring appeal.

Each of us has our very personal way of looking at landscape, and for each of us the same piece of landscape can mean different things at different times. The more intimately we become involved with a bit of countryside—whether it is a granitic Dartmoor upland or scrubby fields whose hedgerows are cluttered with rusty bedsteads on the edge of a city—the richer the experience becomes. At first it is visual, but as we get to know it better, the senses of smell, sound and feeling complicate our perceptions. Familiarity breeds affection. The natural world enriches our emotional lives in a way which scientific and economic analysis cannot measure.

Human beings are incorrigible searchers for meaning and we use the environment as an endless source of symbols. Soil becomes a symbol of permanence; air and water of cleanliness: eagles of freedom; seals of helplessness. This symbolic use of elements within the landscape varies between countries and cultures. In Norway, for example, the spruce stands for home and untrampled nature, while to the British it is an emblem of the undesirable 'alien' and the Kafkaesque power of the forestry industry. The oak is the symbol of national identity for the English, for the Scots it is heather, and for the Welsh the daffodil. Many objects in nature are given meanings and frequently we see animals and plants as symbols of our own potentialities and weaknesses. The lion represents virility and courage, the snake deviousness and spite.

We should not be embarrassed to admit the power of symbols. British conservationists have nearly always justified their hatred of the Sitka spruce in scientific terms. They point out, for instance, that native trees like the oak and willow harbour much larger populations of insects: over two hundred species of insect are associated with oak in Britain; fewer than fifty with the alien spruce. But wouldn't it be more honest for most of us to say that the oak—like Magna Carta, fish and chips, Shakespeare and intemperate weather— means something special to the British, while the Sitka spruce does not?

The association of events, people, paintings and so on with particular landscapes also endows them with a meaning and importance beyond economic or scientific evaluation. The Lake District is associated with Wordsworth, Beatrix Potter and Arthur Ransome; the moors to the west of Bradford with the Brontës; the Norfolk Broads with Cotman and other water-colourists; Wessex with Thomas Hardy; the downland round Dartford with the eighteenth-century botanists and Darwin; Culloden and Hastings with famous battles. In fact there is probably no valley or hill or plain which doesn't have historical or literary associations which influence the way we see it. Indeed associations with the past are becoming more frequent, more intimate and more compelling as the school of landscape history founded by W. G. Hoskins and the contemporary wave of new archae-ologists and their popularisers open our eyes wider still. But myths and legends are no less forceful than facts. Think, for example, of Sherwood Forest. We do not know whether there was such a person as Robin Hood. This does not matter. The legend has captured the imagination of millions because various trees and caves have been unscientifically linked to the story of Robin Hood and his merry men. The Major Oak, which stands at the heart of the forest, is also known as Robin Hood's tree, although, even if he existed, he could never have seen it as the tree is only five hundred years old. But every year tens of thousands of people come to see the Major Oak, more for its associations than its spectacular size.

A PLACE FOR THE ANIMALS

Most people now accept that other men and women different from ourselves have a right to manage their own affairs. Such was not the case a century ago, when our predecessors were busy exploring the globe and exploiting people they saw as 'savages' for their own commercial profit. We persist in treating animals much as our forebears did the natives of Africa.

In moral philosophy rights are understood to form a coherent system: no one has a right to do to another what that other has a right not to have done to it, even though one may have an interest in doing something which the other may wish to resist. This formula derives from the philosophy of Immanuel Kant, who rationalised his devotion to human interests by insisting that non-humans could only be tools and material for human use. He maintained that animals could not have goals of their own. If we abandon the arbitrary line which Kant drew round the human species and include other creatures, can his system of rights work within the larger context, where the land is seen as a community where moral agents have moral duties?

Obviously, most members of such a community are in no position to realise moral duties. And whether one likes it or not, nature is 'red in tooth and claw': there are frequent conflicts of interest between members of the community. However, this does not necessarily make the community model unusable. There can be no general right to live without being hurt or killed, or to be protected from starvation and disease, because to protect it in some creatures would be to deny it in others. The worm has no right not to be killed. And the blackbird injures no right by killing the worm for her basic needs, though she would do so if she in some way conspired to make it impossibly difficult for other species to live out their programmes and to enjoy their time (metaphorically, one assumes, in the case of the worm) under the sun. It is not unjust to kill if we must do so to survive. It is unjust, however, if we humans plot to cover the whole world with our machines and *objets d'art* without remembering the claims of other creatures.

Paradoxically, in view of what we have said about scientific conservation, the ideal which we might pursue is one that lives up to the demands of ecologists for variety. The argument that diversity of species ensures environmental stability, which was once considered a good thing by some ecologists, has been rejected now by most scientists of repute. This makes no odds. A diverse environment is desirable precisely because it means other creatures are being allowed their place in the scheme of things. Just as our predecessors were slowly brought to realise that natives of other continents were not simply a resource to be used, but members of the human community, so should we acknowledge that the health and happiness of other creatures are themselves a good reason for not shooting them, not polluting rivers, not destroying woodlands and not poisoning the atmosphere. We should do more than spare animals pain. We should accept that their rights may prevent us justly achieving all our goals. They are our evolutionary relatives, and like us they know neither where they came from nor where they are going. We can sympathise with many of their desires and feelings, and even when we can't, only anthropocentric conceit will assert that our concerns are more important than theirs.

Animal rights campaigners have tended to concentrate on domestic animals, and they have undoubtedly raised the emotional temperature of the debate about our obligations towards them. What are these obligations?

Alongside the general duty to respect the autonomy of our fellow human beings, there are more specific and local duties to care for one another and to obey laws justly made within the framework of whatever form of social contract we are party to. Although no human community ever began with an explicit bargain to play fair being struck between its members, we can assess the present state of the human group by asking whether its members would rationally have consented to the bargain under which they live: do they all stand to gain, in whatever terms they prefer? All of us, for example, stand to gain from the maintenance of a civil community in which disputes are resolved by unbiased courts. We may lose occasionally, but almost all of us would lose far more if we lived in a state of nature where a handful of the strong overwhelmed a majority of the weaker.

Can there be a social contract, similar to that which exists between humans, between humans and animals? It does not matter how humans came to domesticate animals, although it is worth remarking that it is probably this long history of co-operation with animals that has given us the capacity to sympathise with them. Perhaps dogs and people really did recognise mutual advantages in their co-operation: but even if they didn't, and if the first domestic dogs were strictly captive and saleable commodities, it is still illuminating and instructive to hypothesise a contract. (We recognise, of course, that strictly speaking a contract can only exist between consenting parties who accept interlocking obligations to one another.) As a cautionary fable we can suggest that humans, horses, dogs and cattle began by co-operating. Humans provided the skills of forethought, and the animals returned the compliment by providing assistance, companionship, transport, milk, clothing and meat. This notional contract could be easily manipulated by humans. Because the strength is ours, it is we who are obliged to enforce the contract upon ourselves. There is clearly a powerful drive towards treating animals first as unequal partners and then as chattels, deprived of contractual rights.

We suggest that our practices should be assessed by referring to what might be rationally acceptable to all parties. It is debatable whether it would be rational of cattle to accept care and fodder on condition that their male calves be culled to feed the carers; but cattle might prefer to be looked after and lose their calves than be left to the mercy of wolves. No-one, however, could suggest that it would be rational of cattle to accept intensive farming and all the cruelty it entails. Whether or not one believes animals to have rights, and regardless of whether one believes it possible for a notional social contract to exist between thinking, moralising man and non-philosophising animals, we do have obligations to treat animals decently and to accept that their claims to life must impose restraints on our activities, both on the farm and off.

It is relatively easy to make such a notional contract stick between men and domestic animals. The good they do for us and the care we can provide for them are obvious, and these are the building blocks of the deal. Things become harder when we seek to apply the same sort of contractual framework to relations with wild animals. 'Caring' and 'duty' seem out of place in a state of rude nature. A domesticated dog is trained not to kill sheep, but to round them up at human command. In so doing he performs his part of the contract with man. The wolf can hardly be asked to do the same. Even if possible, it would not be a very efficient use of the species and, more important, would be a derogation of the very wildness that we value in the wolf.

Wildness is indeed the key to the problem of the rights of wild animals. They share the planet with us and, although we do not direct their lives as we do those of domestic beasts, we benefit from their presence and activities in all sorts of ways. Just as we benefit from being able to enjoy untamed countryside and from being able to adventure into a wilderness, so we are intellectually and aesthetically refreshed by the sight and knowledge of wild animals co-existing with ourselves.

They perform innumerable environmental tasks for which we are always indebted to them. Darwin called earthworms 'the ploughs of God'; it is we who benefit from the fertile tilth they create.

CONSERVATION—A MINORITY CONCERN?

The economist John Kenneth Galbraith claimed that "the conservationist is a man who concerns himself with the beauties of nature in roughly inverse proportion to the number of people who can enjoy it". And he berated conservationists for "rising up in awesome anger...at a proposal...to desecrate some unknown stream in some obscure corner of some remote national park". Sadly, Galbraith has a point: conservationists have sometimes been as guilty of selfishness and elitism as the landowners they attack. We must establish not just why we conserve nature, but for whom.

Some conservationists, playing on the mystique of science, have invoked 'scientific' ideas to keep others off the land. The NCC, particularly in its early years, had a habit of acquiring nature reserves and promptly denying public access to them. This form of protectionism, with the government scientists jealously guarding parcels of land for their own ill-defined purposes, perpetuated the lie that the non-scientific laity could not be trusted in the countryside; a lie which many landowners, albeit for different reasons, have been happy to subscribe to. It did nothing for the image of conservation, which came to be seen by many as an indulgence available only for the few.

While some have periodically used science to suit their own narrow purposes, others have used conservation as a flag of convenience in their battles against developments which they considered undesirable for reasons that had little to do with conservation. Consider, for example, the people of Luddesdown, a small village in Kent. In the 1970s a long-distance footpath—the Wealdway—was planned to run from Gravesend to the south coast. The inhabitants of Luddesdown made a tremendous fuss, claiming that the footpath would bring with it hordes of ramblers who would disturb the peace. Some years later the Ministry of Defence announced that it wanted Bowling Alley, a lovely valley beside Luddesdown. The villagers were rightly outraged. But—surprise, surprise—the villagers now claimed that if the MoD took the land it would ruin a valuable amenity—that same footpath which they had so bitterly opposed a few years earlier.

We could dredge up dozens of examples to show how conservation arguments and ecological red herrings have been used by one section of the community to thwart another. In general, it has been the wealthier middle classes seeking to protect their own interests, often to the detriment of less articulate and poorer neighbours. There is an irony here, as conservationists have periodically attempted to link environmental conservation with humanitarian aims such as alleviating poverty. It has been claimed by some that there is a direct relationship between nature conservation and economic development, and that the latter, which is the key to solving malnutrition and poverty, cannot succeed without the former. This is thoroughly disingenuous, if not plain dishonest. Is there any reason to believe that the security of food production in Ethiopia has anything to do with the conservation of wildlife? Would African food production suffer if the lion and the elephant and the giraffe disappeared? Of course not. Wherever sham philanthropy is marshalled in defence of the natural world, the moral status of animals, and our moral resposibilities towards them, are, by implication, denied. There are perfectly good reasons—we have mentioned many of them already—why the wildlife of Ethiopia should be conserved: to say that it is for the sake of the hungry and destitute is to play on their misfortune.

So we have some sympathy for Galbraith's views. But to tar all conservationists with the same brush would be unfair. Indeed, we do have an interest in conserving the countryside, its scenery and wildlife. But it is a collective interest. Whatever we do to protect nature, and to ensure that domestic animals are well treated, must be for the sake of not just a few, but for all of us.

To sum up. The ideal to which we look, without exaggerated optimism, is a countryside in which humans manage their activities—agricultural, recreational, scientific, whatever—in such a way as to allow the maximum possible use of the land to other creatures. Farm animals should be regarded as partners, paying their way and being given in return care and affection. It has always been difficult to manage the delicate emotional strategy of caring for a creature upon which one later intends to feast. But as the message slowly sinks in, that we are not of a radically different kind, we can look forward to the day when the contract of mutual profit will be redefined. Many creatures will be bred back to their wild state, to be hunted by other creatures perhaps, but no longer expected to feel gratitude for being enslaved. That is a long-term goal. Meanwhile, it will be enough to allow the wild things their place, and to give the tame what they are owed, in terms of a life well-lived. That, after all, is the bargain each of us might rationally have made: to live as members of our civil community at the price of being asked, some day, to die for it.

CHAPTER THREE

A Countryside for People

A Countryside
for People

PUBLIC debate about the countryside has been so dominated by environmental issues in recent years that at times it has seemed as though the countryside consisted only of farmers and wildlife—a landscape strangely denuded of the people who live and work in it. There have been outcries—quite rightly—about disappearing orchids and otters, but governments have shown little interest in disappearing farm-workers, the increasing rural unemployment and the steady decline in public services in villages.

The countryside has always been in a state of flux. There have been the periods of great drama—such as the enclosure of commons and the Highland clearances—but between these great events the social structure and the patterns of land-use were also changing, though less obviously. Throughout the last few hundred years there has been no shortage of essayists and poets keen to document the changing countryside. Few have resisted the temptation to look back nostalgically to the 'good old days', but the old days were not so good for most country dwellers, either in the near or distant past. The cart driver in Constable's *The Hay Wain* probably lived in a hovel, survived on a diet of bread and potatoes, sired children who died in the cot or soon after, and worked seventy odd hours a week for a wage insufficient to feed and clothe his family decently. Raymond Williams, in his classic study *The Country and the City* (London, 1973), believes that the first problem, when looking at social change, is one of perspective. He singles out an author who asserted in 1932 that the 'organic community' of 'Old England' had only recently disappeared. He then turns his attention to Sturt, who was writing at the beginning of this century. "Sturt traced this ending [of the old English community] to two periods: enclosure after 1861 and residential settlement after 1900. Yet this at once takes us into the period of Thomas Hardy's novels, written between 1871 and 1896 and referring to rural England since the 1830s. And had not the critics insisted that it was here, in Hardy, that we found the record of the great climacteric change in rural life: the disturbance and destruction of what one writer has called the 'timeless rhythm of agriculture and the seasons'?"

Then Williams cites Cobbett, who was looking back "to the happier country, the Old England of his boyhood, during the 1770s and 1780s". And, as we creep back through time, we find no lack of writers recalling the better times; and the better times, with few exceptions, coincided with their youth. "Against sentimental and intellectualized accounts of an unlocalized 'Old England'," warned Williams, "we need, evidently, the sharpest scepticism." We agree. We have no wish to recreate the 'good old days', or to ask the farm-worker once again to experience the dreadful drudgery of those many jobs like hoeing sugar beet which machines now do. We are concerned with revitalising the countryside. Something must be done, and done quickly, about the shortage of housing, the decline of public transport and the loss of jobs which have trapped many indigenous country-dwellers in isolated poverty, ignored by most local authorities and seldom considered by any political party. We must also create the opportunities for the less affluent town-dwellers to move into the countryside and to work in it if they wish.

With a few minor qualifications, the changing nature of rural society is rooted in the changes which have taken place in agriculture. The truth is that agriculture is now only of residual economic significance in most of the countryside. The latest detailed figures come from a 1984 government survey, which found that only 14.1 per cent of those employed in rural areas were involved in agriculture. The construction industry (all the figures here are for rural employment) accounted for 7.5 per cent of the work force, while nearly 20 per cent were involved in manufacturing. Distribution and catering, with 18.1 per cent, and 'other services', with 32.3 per cent, far exceeded agricultural employment. The forestry industry (both state and private sectors) frequently cites the employment potential of woodland management as a reason why it should be generously funded out of the public purse, but the trends for forestry have, in recent decades, been similar to those in farming: per hectare employment has rapidly declined. Employment in recreation and tourism, in contrast, has experienced a phenomenal growth since the last war, though the numbers involved remain small.

The transformation of rural villages into non-agricultural settlements has been mainly a matter of transport mobility. Commuting by train from the Home Counties to jobs in London (and, to a lesser extent, from similar zones around other conurbations) was fast developing before the First World War. It continued with further electrification of the railways in the 1920s and 1930s and was promoted after the Second World War by the relative cheapness, until the late 1960s, of country real estate, which attracted an overwhelmingly professional and managerial commuting population into the countryside. In the 1960s and 1970s the building of motorways and the widespread ownership of cars in the middle and upper classes combined to commuterise villages lying off and between the major radial routes. Only a few rural areas, isolated by bad roads and the lack of railways, remained relatively untouched by the process. By virtue of that isolation they were gobbled up instead by the voracious demand for holiday homes and weekend cottages.

The newcomers, like the majority of landowners and farmers, are not particularly bothered by the absence of essential services such as shops or schools in the village; they can hop into their cars and drive to the supermarkets, schools and dispensaries of the nearest town. Nor do they have problems finding a place in which to live or they wouldn't have moved into the countryside. In contrast, there is a rump of the depleted local working population tied to one place by low-paid employment, by unemployment, by old age, and by the lack of money which would enable them to move. The material conditions of the poor have considerably improved in absolute terms since the last war; but in relative terms they have made little, if any progress, and in recent years they have fallen back.

So who is to blame? Certainly not the newcomers. After all, most people, given the opportunity, migrate to the environment in which they most wish to live. Nor can one blame those who have suffered most—the poor—for not improving their lot. For an answer, we must look at government policies. What we now witness is an ironic outcome of the system of town and country planning created by the legislation of the immediate post-war period. Its commitment was to contain the spread of urban sprawl across the countryside and to maintain 'socially balanced communities'. In practice, the efforts put into the first of these aims have far outweighed the second, and the pursuit of urban containment has been directly responsible for creating 'unbalanced communities'. The irony lies in the fact that the underlying political aims of planning policy were liberal, progressive and sometimes even utopian: a Fabian desire to eradicate the worst irrationalities of industrial and residential development by radical reform of the laissez-faire approach to land-use. The blueprints of the 1940s contained a strong element of planning for the least fortunate; but in practice it has been the privileged members of rural society who have benefited most from the operation of the planning system. The poor have gained little.

Planning policy was originally defined in terms of land-use (zoning, design, development control and so forth), and attempts to relate these objectives to the social needs of the rural population have been sporadic. Social policy in the countryside was translated into protecting it from urban sprawl and providing (limited) public services. It was quite wrongly believed that this would help to retain the 'traditional rural way of life'. There was no attempt to find out how the policies might affect the distribution of resources and opportunities within the rural population. The belief was that the countryside should be preserved almost exclusively for agriculture—and this at a time when farming was already shedding labour at an alarming rate. Industrial development was therefore directed away from the countryside. The planners' notion that towns had industry, and the countryside did not, became more and more firmly established. The obsession with containment kept house-building to an inadequate minimum—in both the public and private sectors—and a planned scarcity of rural housing duly emerged. Public housing in rural areas is now in chronically short supply, as is cheap private housing. Inevitably, it is a shortage that has been most keenly felt among the low-paid.

Although many people spoke out against the shortcomings of the rural planning system in the 1970s, it was too late to stop the rot. The newcomers had their own interests and, having sought and found their rustic retreats, they firmly resisted new industrial and housing developments. Indeed, they had been attracted to country life by the very absence of developments which might have helped the poor and deprived. For newcomers, more local jobs and houses detracted from, rather than enhanced, the quality of rural life. Well-informed and articulate, they soon made their presence felt in local decision-making and, when faced with the prospect of a new factory or council-house development, they usually—and generally successfully—objected.

Over the last forty years we have seen the gradual run-down of a whole range of public services in the countryside. In some cases, policies pursued in both urban and rural areas, for example closing smaller schools as rolls have fallen or educational fashion has changed, have had disproportionately severe effects on rural communities. Nor is it only changes in public services that have had particularly serious consequences for such areas; the development of hyper-markets and new shopping centres has not been matched in rural areas, as it has in many urban centres, by the growth in 'open all hours' corner shops. Village shops and post offices, like village schools and village doctors, have disappeared in droves. (We concentrate in this book mainly on rural transport and rural housing, but a similar story of decline touches many other areas too.)

The rail network has been severely pruned. In 1963 there were just under seventeen thousand miles of rail. Twenty years later less than two-thirds were still in use. In 1963 British Rail had four thousand two hundred stations. Now there are fewer than two and a half thousand. Rural bus services have also been axed. Between 1971 and 1982 the National Bus Company cut its mileage by nearly a quarter, and most of the lost miles were in the countryside. (Deregulation, which we discuss further on, is making matters worse). No other European country has such a dismal record of cutting bus services as Britain. During the decade 1971-81, the number of bus and coach travellers increased by 135 per cent in Italy, 55 per cent in France and 41 per cent in Denmark. In only two countries did numbers decline: in Belgium by 2 per cent and in Britain by a massive 17 per cent. For those without a car these cuts in public transport have made the loss of the village shop, school and local surgery all the harder to bear.

Public services have clearly suffered from the self-reliance of the newcomers, and the less well-off, now in a minority, find it more and more difficult to make government acknowledge their needs. The majority of rate-payers are reluctant to foot the rapidly rising bill for servicing their less fortunate neighbours, and they choose, quite democratically, to accept lower levels of taxation. For the poor no choice exists. Many have not consciously chosen to remain in their community: they have been stranded by social and economic forces over which they have no control, and by growing public indifference. Not that such deprivation is anything new. The history of most villages is one of poverty. But in the past, poverty was at least the norm, and the experience of it was shared by most of the village. Now poverty brings with it a sense of exclusion rather than mutuality.

The planning system is essentially a tool of the rural 'haves' who dominate county and district councils. They have no wish to redress these social imbalances. But even if policies were recast in a way which made social needs as central as land-use to planning policies, the balance of political forces in the countryside would still be against their enthusiastic implementation. In urging a better deal for the deprived, we must establish both how a more equitable distribution of resources can be achieved, and how this can be done without recourse to draconian powers which over-ride local sentiment (which means, whether we like it or not, acknowledging the views of the affluent majority).

A WORKING COUNTRYSIDE

The message that work can and should be dignified is one to which we all subscribe, yet in this country politicians of all hues, with a few notable exceptions, continue to view those without work as little more than potential cogs in a system of production. One politician who has challenged the orthodox presumption that people are made for production, rather than the other way round, is the Labour MP Robin Cook. Reflecting on the 'Alternative Economic Strategy' of some of his colleagues, Cook decried its unequivocal call for exponential growth and asked: "What would be the diseconomies of such 'steady and sustained' growth? How much more pollution? How much faster the depletion of natural resources that cannot be replaced? How much further dehumanisation of the labour process in the relentless search for greater output?" It is extraordinary, as Cook said, that the debate over the return to full employment has never got beyond the question of how we could create the necessary number of jobs to examine which jobs would provide "sufficient sense of reward to make them worth creating".

The countryside may not be able to provide millions of new jobs, but by its very nature it can provide jobs which endow the worker with "real riches, which are not the riches of money but of leisure and creation". Indeed, many who work in the countryside put the quality of work above monetary gain as a reason for continuing an often hard life. A 1983 survey of small farmers found that incomes were very low. Of the four hundred and twenty seven interviewed, less than a quarter made more than £5,000 a year, and over a quarter earned less than £1,000. Yet these were full-time farmers who chose to continue farming, and they gave two reasons for doing so. First, they enjoyed living in the countryside. Second, they enjoyed the variety and interest of their work. Our message is a simple one: let us create as many jobs as we can in the countryside, but let us ensure that they are jobs from which people will derive satisfaction and pride. Nobody is suggesting the re-creation of an impoverished peasantry. But we should not countenance the seduction of people into futile and boring jobs by the promise of money and nothing else.

Between 1960 and 1986 the number of farming jobs was halved, whilst during the same period the number of manufacturing jobs in rural Britain increased by well over one hundred thousand. The prospects for some further creation of jobs in manufacturing industries in rural areas are reasonable, given sensible planning policies, not least because affluent newcomers have created a market for certain kinds of goods—mostly of high quality and produced on a small scale. Many regional and national companies, attracted by a pool of cheap (and often female) labour and keen to take advantage of the improved motorway-network, have located their units in small towns. However, the recent recession has shown that many of these businesses are vulnerable to closure during a period of economic retrenchment and rationalisation, and it would be foolish to suggest that manufacturing employment in rural areas will show anything more than a slight absolute rise over coming years.

The service sector offers better prospects for economic growth in the countryside. It is already the largest source of employment in most rural areas and it is the sector which is already generating most jobs nationally. The affluent majority of the rural population, as one would expect, presents a large and growing market for the service economy.

Information technology will undoubtedly play a crucial role in the future of rural areas. The potential of modern information-technology to overcome the constraints of isolation and distance is yet to be fully realised, but we can envisage that for the first time since the Industrial Revolution rural areas will participate in far-reaching technological breakthroughs as fully as urban centres. New information-technologies may help provide new sources of employment in rural areas, but the pace and direction of changes introduced by such technology will be as much a product of the social context within which they are applied as of mere invention or availability. New technologies will not eradicate the social polarisation of rural communities. Indeed, they will probably make things worse.

We can be much clearer about the prospects for employment in land management, and much happier about the benefits, in terms of satisfaction, that such jobs will give. There is an enormous potential, already being realised in some areas, albeit on a small scale, for jobs in nature conservation, habitat management and recreation.

Forty years ago there was no such thing as a 'job in conservation'. However, a recent study by the NCC identified over fourteen thousand people involved in some sort of conservation work. These include sixteen hundred working for 'mainstream bodies' such as the NCC itself, the RSPB and county naturalists' trusts. A further one thousand seven hundred and forty work for bodies such as the National Trust and two Countryside Commissions (there is one for England and Wales, and another for Scotland), which are partially involved in nature conservation. Central and local government accounts for about one hundred specialised jobs.

In the past few years many of the county naturalists' trusts have taken advantage of the Manpower Services Commission (MSC) community programme scheme, and they have shown that the countryside provides huge potential for satisfying jobs. For example, BBONT (Berks, Bucks and Oxon Naturalists' Trust) has taken on over eighty young unemployed people over the past year in the south Oxfordshire area alone. Some have been involved in habitat surveys, others in coppicing woodland, fencing, tree-planting, creating paths, administration and digging and clearing ponds. Some participants, having worked with the scheme for a year or so, have moved on to permanent employment, having gained new expertise in countryside management. The cost of employing eighty people per year at BBONT works out at around £250,000. In 1984 over five hundred people were employed on similar schemes in eighteen naturalists' trusts. This is just a fraction of the numbers who could be employed in the countryside, and the scheme has shown the potential that exists for creating permanent, productive new jobs. At a rough estimate, we could expect to see fifty thousand jobs created in this field over the next five years—at a cost to the government of just £250 million per year. This would not include the tens of thousands of jobs which will be created in the 'land bank' we advocate.

A radical restructuring of the farming industry will also create many more jobs. Expanded local authority smallholdings will get many thousands onto the land, and we can expect to see part-time farming assuming much greater significance. Already somewhere between forty and sixty per cent of farm holdings are run by people who derive more than half their income from other sources. MAFF treats part-time farmers with disdain (as does the National Farmers' Union) and for most farm development schemes, units which are not capable of supporting full-time workers for more than 1,800 hours a year are ineligible for grant-aid. This makes no sense. We should be encouraging more part-timers. For many people, part-time farming, combined with another form of employment, whether computer-programming, factory work or whatever, provides the best of both worlds. In Bavaria, special efforts are made to ensure that new businesses are integrated with the employment needs of the part-time farmer. The same should happen here.

It is also clear that many small farmers could increase their earning capacity either by adding value to farm produce (for example by turning milk into cheese, EEC quotas allowing, making bread or preparing poultry for sale) or by catering for the increasing demand for recreation and holiday accommodation. In marginal areas such as the uplands many farms run thriving bed-and-breakfast businesses. With a little ingenuity and encouragement, a family could make a living on a very small area of land.

HOUSING

We must ensure that an adequate stock of decent housing, at a reasonable price, is made available for those who live and work in the countryside. Over recent decades there has been a steady reduction in private rented accommodation and there is a chronic shortage of local authority housing in rural areas. A recently completed survey underlined the huge gap between the rich and the poor in rural areas. In 1981, seventy-five per cent of all rural households in council housing, and sixty-three per cent in private rented accommodation, had net incomes below £6,000 p.a. The survey also found that around fifty per cent of typical first-time-buyer houses in rural areas cost more than £30,000, compared to five per cent nationally. Since the late 1960s house prices have risen dramatically and local people have been unable to compete with commuters and those retiring to the countryside. The ownership of second homes and holiday cottages has worsened the situation, and restrictive planning policies have effectively halted developments on the outskirts of small towns and villages.

Housing policy in Britain has been almost exclusively geared to solving the problems of urban areas, and government, both central and local, has ignored housing shortages in the countryside. Recent pressure has again increased on green-field sites where 'volume developers' want to build houses for commuters. In contrast, we want to build low-cost housing and housing for rent in existing small villages and towns.

The Socialist Countryside Group (SCG) has proposed that Housing Stress Areas (HSAs) should be designated in rural Britain, and that they should operate in the same way as the Housing Action Areas/General Improvement Areas which were introduced under the 1974 Housing Act. This makes good sense. Under the HSA programme local authorities would identify areas where the housing stock needs to be protected for local people. The Department of the Environment should adopt a stick-and-carrot approach to local authorities. Real incentives would be given to the local authorities which used the HSA procedures, and those which ignored the needs of local people by failing to implement HSA schemes could be penalised through the 'block granting' system. The DoE would independently assess local needs, and local authorities ignoring these would be spurred into action by central government. If they remained recalcitrant, voluntary housing associations would be given the opportunity to build in HSAs.

The main principle of the HSA programme would be to restrict sales of both existing and new properties to local people if there is sufficient demand. The local authority will intervene in the housing market to depress prices where necessary. The HSA programme could be further bolstered by other measures:

• Building for Sale: Local authorities should continue to enter into agreements with local contractors, the Housing Corporation, housing associations and so on, both within and outside HSAs. The Development Commission and the Housing Corporation should be encouraged to concentrate as much as possible on HSAs, where the housing need is greatest. In addition, local authority building schemes should be encouraged and carried out either by the council itself, or through local partnership agreements. Local building contractors should always be favoured above those from outside. The HSA system would provide finance for local authorities to build and sell houses, but the councils should always retain a right of repurchase.

• Building for Rent: Councils would be encouraged to initiate a programme of building for rent. At present caravan-dwellers and tenants of tied accommodation are not allowed onto the housing lists of local authorities. In future, they must be.

• Rating Policy: Some of the HSA programme would be financed through local rates. There should be compulsory rating of all empty housing, and there should be a graduated system whereby rates rise the longer a property remains unoccupied. We also believe that rates on second homes should be higher than for permanently occupied properties. We would expect to see the number of second homes in rural areas gradually diminish. Higher rates for second homes would bring some extra income into the local authorities' coffers, but the policy's real aim would be to reduce second-home ownership. However, some of the money for new council-house building should come from the rating of agricultural land, which we deal with in the next section. (Of course, current moves to replace rates by a poll tax will make matters worse, and most second-home owners will presumably make no contribution to the rural economy).

• Compulsory Purchase: Compulsory purchase should be used as a last resort to take over empty houses in HSAs. Whatever housing was acquired in this way would join the stock of local council housing.

REVIVING PUBLIC TRANSPORT

According to the advertisements, 'This is the age of the train'. It is not. And nor is it the age of the bus. If any form of transport deserves the accolade it is the car.

In 1985 almost forty per cent of British households had no regular use of a car and only thirty-one per cent of women over seventeen years old could drive. Nevertheless, the number of cars on the road has increased by twenty-five per cent over the last decade—most of this increase being from households that already possessed one car. The use of buses and coaches has plummeted, fares have risen and services have been cut. Rail fares in Britain are much higher than in most European countries and the services are among the worst. Central government has happily allowed the rail system to be run down, and between 1976 and 1982 the subsidy to British Rail was cut (in real terms) by forty-six per cent. Sweden, with a population one seventh of ours, spends almost as much on its rail service as we do. West Germany spends six times more. (The purchase of company cars costs Britain almost £2,000 million in lost revenue every year—a figure somewhat greater than the combined subsidies for train and bus services.)

The situation is particularly serious in rural areas, where those on low wages or none at all, and those unable or unwilling to drive or suffering from disabilities, depend for mobility entirely on public transport. Over the last few years we have seen many innovative schemes which have proved beyond all doubt that good public transport attracts people away from their cars. For example, in 1982 London Transport introduced a combined tube and bus 'Travelcard'. In its first year this generated an extra £60 million in income and use of both buses and tubes shot up, by thirteen per cent and forty-four per cent respectively. Some local authorities in rural areas have established community minibus schemes and these too have been successful. Unfortunately, the government has decided that all the problems of rural bus provision could be solved by deregulation and privatisation.

Deregulation involves the abolition of planned bus services and the creation of a 'free market'. But a free market can only work where there are enough would-be consumers to create competition—this is manifestly not so in rural public transport.

It is vital that rural bus services be maintained and improved. We are opposed unreservedly to deregulation of bus services and to their privatisation, and we believe that the interests of those without a car can be best served by a variety of means: by expanding bus services where reasonable demand exists; by subsidising minibus schemes; and, in the areas where demand is lowest, by introducing a 'taxi-token' system.

Let us look, briefly, at the last of our three suggestions. We believe that pensioners and those without work or on low incomes should be entitled to a monthly allowance of taxi tokens. These tokens would be provided by the local authority, and taxi drivers would be able to exchange the tokens for the fare price. Obviously the value of the tokens will vary according to distance travelled. They will enable people living in remote areas without buses to visit shops, health centres and so on with reasonable regularity. We would expect most taxi services to be privately owned, but some might be owned and run by local authorities. In each rural area the taxi service would soon establish a list of customers, and it would be able to arrange to pick up a full car-load, or minibus-load, for each journey. Services would run at a frequency which reflected local needs, and to a timetable determined by the customers.

Here we come to the question of finance. Where will the money come from to pay for better public transport, and for that matter, for more local authority house-building and improvements in other public services like education? Such is the importance of improving both public housing and transport that there is a strong argument in favour of central government being more generous in its allocation of subsidy for these purposes. However, if we search for a new source of revenue we need look no further than the countryside itself. At present farmland is exempted from rates. This anomalous situation should be no longer tolerated. Before Mrs Thatcher abolished the government's Think Tank on 'Reducing Agricultural Subsidies', it calculated that the rating of agricultural land would raise £400 million a year. This is a colossal sum, and we believe that some of it should be channelled into maintaining and improving public transport in and to the countryside, into new house-building programmes in HSAs and into other public services. There will be some farmers, particularly those on poor land with small acreages and those managing their land for conservation and recreation, who will be unable to afford the land rates. There should be, therefore, a system of exemptions and rebates, such as exists in the housing sector. The rating of agricultural land provides us with a tremendous opportunity to finance and improve public services, and the benefit will be particularly felt by that very group of people who have suffered most from the social polarisation which we discussed at the beginning of this chapter.

By the end of this century we would like to see a countryside in which the main means of getting about will be by public transport—train, bus, collective taxi, perhaps even by canal barge. Fewer cars on the road will mean less pollution; and more people out of cars will mean better public services. We hope that traffic on existing roads will decline, and we unreservedly oppose the building of any new motorways.

HEALTH AND EDUCATION

In the provision of health and education services, the countryside has fared particularly badly and the more remote a village and the smaller it is, the worse the situation. The number of children receiving nursery education is ten per cent below the national average in rural areas. A 1981 survey found that no state-financed nursery education existed in rural Gloucestershire, and only two per cent of three- and four-year-old children in Norfolk were provided with nursery education. As far as health services are concerned, the last few decades have seen the closure of many cottage hospitals, and a survey by the National Federation of Women's Institutes found that fifty-four per cent of villages had no doctor's surgery, seventy-five per cent had no chemist and eighty-four per cent had no dentist. Again those who have suffered most have been the old, the handicapped and the poor.

As the countryside becomes revitalised, with many more people not just living in it but working in it, we expect such services to increase again. However, in the meantime, local authorities should help voluntary groups to establish such facilities as nurseries and community health projects where today they do not exist. Central government should finance local initiatives where local authorities fail to do so.

CHAPTER FOUR

Opening Up
the Countryside

Opening Up the Countryside

THE LAWS which restrict where we can go in the countryside are founded on the belief that people are not to be trusted. It is presumed that the vast mass of Britain's inhabitants, once off the roads and out of their cars will follow a course of selfish destruction; if we are given the freedom to go where we choose, we shall abuse it. This is the line taken by such organisations as the National Farmers' Union (NFU) and the Country Landowners' Association (CLA), yet damage done to crops, farm stock and commercial forestry is on such a small scale that it is hard to find any quantifiable evidence of it.

There may be the occasional problem—for example, gates left open may allow sheep and cattle to stray, and dogs occasionally harrass and kill sheep. But, if anything, the walker is at much greater risk from farming operations than farming operations from the walker. Nevertheless, many landowners persist in championing the myth that townspeople pose a threat to their activities, and as a result such provisions as have been made in legislation for public access have been largely negative and almost invariably miserly. At present, a visitor to the countryside, looking over a gate, will wonder, 'Am I allowed in there?' We must fight for a position where the walker knows that he or she is allowed 'in there'—unless a properly authorised prohibition is in force. At the moment access (on foot or otherwise) is the exception. It must become the rule.

In the countryside of England and Wales we have about one hundred thousand miles of footpaths, and these vary from tiny paths threading through village fields, between schools and farm cottages, to long-distance footpaths which cover hundreds of miles. A spokesperson for the NFU once made the rash statement that these footpaths took up five hundred thousand acres of good land, and that if this land was producing food it would feed half a million people. This calculation was based on an assumption that footpaths were both fertile and forty feet wide. Whatever the acreage, it is surely better that this land should be used for recreation than surplus production. Even if we doubled the acreage in footpaths, it would only make a small dent in the grain mountain.

The battle for freedom of access to open country—moors, fells, downs and heaths—has been going on for over a century. The first major access bill was laid before Parliament in 1884, and many more followed. However, it wasn't until 1949, when the Labour government introduced the National Parks and Access to the Countryside Act, that any real progress was made by the access lobby. But even in our national parks (and the equally extensive areas of outstanding natural beauty) much of the country is not subject to public access. The exception is the Peak District National Park, where the public has legal rights of access to forty-five thousand acres.

Spatially, the provision for public access is very uneven. Those who live in the towns of the north and west—providing they have a car—are conspicuously better catered for than those in the south and east. The Peak District National Park is within easy reach of Birmingham, Sheffield and the towns of the West Riding. The Lake District, where *de facto* access exists over much of the fells, is within striking distance of the cities of Lancashire, and in general people who live close to upland farmland, where crops are few and extensive grazing of sheep and cattle predominates, are more fortunate than those surrounded by the intensively cultivated lowlands. Lincolnshire and Norfolk, with their rich soils ideally suited to arable cropping, are exceedingly poorly served by footpaths. In terms of public paths per square mile, they have about half the national average. The situation in the lowlands is getting worse rather than better, largely because of the demands of intensive agriculture. Indeed, the NFU is keen to 'rationalise' the system of footpaths on farmland. For rationalise, read 'reduce'. Many farmers have pulled out hedges and trees to maximise the efficiency of their large machines, and many have ploughed up footpaths which run through their fields, for roughly the same reasons. Numerous reports by the Ramblers' Association over decades have shown how widespread and thoroughgoing this theft of public assets has been. Independent confirmation came in 1984 when a survey of sample parishes by the Countryside Commission found that nearly sixty per cent of paths in arable fields were 'adversely affected' by farming. As the NFU was represented on the steering group for the survey and raised no objection, it can be assumed that it too recognises these facts.

Modern farming operations have also made walking in the countryside a hazardous occupation. Some three per cent of arable land is subject to aerial spraying with pesticides, and spray-drift from tractor-pulled booms may also expose the rambler to a noxious dose of dangerous chemicals. Farmers are well aware of the health risks, and some play safe by illegally erecting 'Keep Out' notices and barbed-wire fences to deter walkers. The 1981 Wildlife and Countryside Act did little to improve access in the countryside. If anything, it worsened affairs by making it legal for farmers to keep bulls in fields with public paths.

It is commonly supposed that public access is better catered for in woods and forests than on farmland. This is often not the case. For example, Oxfordshire has twenty seven thousand acres of woodland, yet the public has access to only one hundred and eleven acres, or about 0.4 per cent. One of the loveliest woods in that county is the thirteen hundred acre Wychwood Forest. The public are allowed into the wood on just one day a year, Palm Sunday. One notes with some sadness that part of Wychwood Forest is managed as a nature reserve by a public body, the Nature Conservancy Council, yet for decades neither it, nor the local authorities, which could make paths by order, have done anything to encourage the owner to share his wood with the rest of us. Only in the summer of 1986 did Oxfordshire County Council resolve to make such an order. This, of course, is being contested.

Woodland landowners who refuse access to their woodlands often do so on the grounds that they are protecting their shooting interest, the supposition being that were the public to roam freely the game birds would not breed so successfully. However, there is little evidence that human presence has much effect on pheasants. And, in any case, these same landowners will almost always be using sprays on their crops which lead to the disappearance of many species, including game birds like the partridge. The owners of grouse moors have also claimed that public access is incompatible with good game management. Studies carried out at the Institute of Terrestrial Ecology show this to be fallacious. The density of grouse on a moor is related to the nutritional quality of heather; it has nothing to do with people walking over their territories. One can only conclude that the shooting argument is a sham: the real reason why many landowners stop the public walking over their moors and through their woods is simply because they don't want them. Xenophobia rules.

THE DEMAND FOR ACCESS

Two hundred years ago most British people lived and worked in the countryside, and their lives were intimately bound up with the land. Today, most live and work in an urban and often unattractive environment, and the countryside has become the place where we can escape from the frenetic and noisy atmosphere of the city streets, from the tedium of industrial production lines and from the cramped conditions in which so many now live. The use of the countryside for pleasure is of profound importance.

Two recent opinion polls emphasised the importance of the countryside's attractiveness and, by implication, its accessibility. A MORI poll, carried out in 1983, asked what factors contributed most to the 'quality of life'. First came safe streets, which were mentioned by 72 per cent of those interviewed. Second came an attractive countryside (mentioned by 53 per cent), followed by an unpolluted atmosphere (51 per cent) and good public transport (46 per cent). More surprising, perhaps, were the findings of a poll carried out by the CLA among its own members. Sixty-nine per cent considered that landscape and scenery were a more important benefit to them than food production.

The Countryside Commission has carried out frequent surveys of who uses the countryside and what they do once there. In 1984, 85 per cent of the general public made at least one trip to the countryside for recreation. By far the most popular active pursuit was walking. The 1984 survey found that 41 per cent of those interviewed had been on a walk of two miles or more (the average distance walked being just under five miles) during the last twelve months, and 21 per cent had done so within the last four weeks. A third had picked their own fruit in the countryside within the last year, and about a quarter had taken part in some sport in the countryside during the last four weeks.

Where people walked was of even greater interest. The

most frequently visited landscapes were woodlands, farms and fields. Heathlands and moors, the habitats one associates with the great mass trespasses of the past, were much less used, which was doubtless a reflection of the long distances which many must travel to reach them. The importance of the cultivated lowlands for recreation is self-evident, and almost half the trips made to the countryside are of twenty miles or less.

As one would expect, there is a hard core of committed country lovers. One fifth of all those interviewed by the Commission in 1984 were members of wildlife, amenity or recreation organisations, and 72 per cent of these people had made a trip into the countryside during the month prior to being interviewed. In contrast, only 48 per cent of the remaining four-fifths had. Indeed, over two-thirds of the trips made were accounted for by just 16 per cent of the population, a figure which reflects social inequities. The rich make twice as many trips to the countryside as do manual workers and the unemployed, for obvious reasons. Over two-thirds of those visiting the countryside go by car, and only one tenth use buses and trains. As the Socialist Countryside Group has pointed out, "The withdrawal of bus and rail services and the escalation of fares has done more than the gamekeepers ever did to prevent people from getting out into the countryside". Our task is therefore twofold. We must fight for the freedom of access to all the countryside. But, equally importantly, we must ensure that those who are presently unable to get to the countryside are given the opportunity to do so. There is little point in us having a beautiful countryside if many do not have the means to enjoy it.

WHOSE COUNTRYSIDE?

Our manifesto is underpinned by the belief that the countryside belongs to all of us. But the conflicts of today are not just between those who own or manage land and those who seek access to it. The limitations on access exacerbate the conflicts between different recreation groups.

Countryside activities fall along a spectrum. At one end are the 'soft' uses—walking, canoeing, mountaineering, rock-climbing and orienteering—whose impact on the landscape is negligible (except in a handful of highly popular places). At the other end are 'hard' activities like motor-cycling, driving 'off-road recreational vehicles', water skiing, hang-gliding and snow-skiing. These latter have much more impact on the environment and on other visitors. Both the British Horse Society and the Ramblers' Association seek a right of access to all common land, but clearly the impact of ten rambling clubs would be vastly less than that of ten groups of pony-trekkers.

One of the most divisive conflicts has been between ramblers and motor-cyclists. Ramblers are fierce advocates of access on foot; but they are equally fierce opponents of activities such as scrambling and riding trail-bikes on green lanes. They argue that motor-cyclists disturb the peace and tranquillity which they are in the countryside to enjoy (though curiously they accept the throbbing of the farm tractor as part of their Arcadia). And they may also argue (with a good deal less evidence) that motor-cycling is a danger to walkers, damages landscape and disturbs wildlife. Nowhere has the ramblers' antipathy to motor-cyclists been more evident than on ancient tracks like the Ridgeway. The ramblers may have the right of it there, where ancient ambience is vital, but it is hard to see how their absolutist arguments could be applied to more than a few places. The motor-cyclists have every right to demand that their needs are satisfied too. After all, there is nothing morally wrong with noise. Some of us find it offensive in certain contexts— that is all.

The sins of the motor-cyclist take up a great deal more debate and resolution time at annual gatherings of the Ramblers' Association than those of horse riders, whose conflicts with the ramblers are far more widespread and common. This hatred of things mechanical in the countryside may well betray class prejudices, with some ramblers seeing themselves as sensitive aesthetes, wandering as lonely as clouds, and their antagonists as working-class yobs. Whatever its reason, it is a divisive conflict, and one which must be tackled. The fracas has much to do with the restrictions of access that force soft and hard users onto the same piece of ground, and we would be doing much to defuse conflicts if we gained a right of access on foot to all the countryside. We must accept that all pursuits have a place, and we must insist that the visitors, whether on foot or horseback or machine, develop a greater tolerance towards one another. At the moment, ramblers and riders don't consider it any part of their business to find room for hang-gliders and water skiers. It is time they did.

The countryside must accommodate the motor-cyclists and other 'hard' activities. But this requires a serious attempt to plan recreation for the countryside overall, which is easier said than done, especially given the piecemeal and largely selfish ownership and management patterns which prevail today. For example, even in a national park as tightly controlled and well planned as the Lake District, the park authority has experienced great difficulty in its recreation planning. It can prevent certain things happening, but even with large portions of the park in the hands of benevolent owners like the National Trust, positive assignment of land for specific purposes is difficult. The Park authority has opposed certain kinds of leisure use, such as water skiing, which it allows only on Windermere. It is right to exclude some hard users. It ought to be possible to plan for them in the adjacent countryside. However, this must be done, at present, by a separate authority working within its own constraints. Over most of Britain the situation is far worse, for reasons already made clear: the overwhelming bulk of the country-side is held and managed for agriculture or forestry, and owners and land managers seldom make any provision for access or recreation, unless they see money in it.

THE RIGHT OF COMMON ACCESS: WHY WE NEED IT

A considerable improvement in the degree of access to the countryside, especially for the softer users, could be achieved within the present system of land ownership and management. We can predict with some confidence that within the next ten years the greater part of our commons, upland grazing land and remaining downland and heaths will be open to the public on foot as of right. Major improvements can and will be won by the access lobby, and with the agricultural industry on the defensive we can reasonably expect that farmers and landowners will behave better in the future than they do now as far as existing rights of way to the countryside are concerned.

But this will not be enough. We must insist on a right of access to all countryside on foot, subject to no damage being done and the privacy of those who live in the countryside being respected. The 'right of common access' already exists in Sweden, where it works well, and there is no reason to suppose that a similar system would not work here. Why do we want it? First, and most obviously, it would result in a massive extension of access. Second, it would engender a great sense of liberation in the countryside, and this would be accompanied by an increasing sense of public responsibility towards the countryside. Refusal of access today is *au fond* a matter of believing that the majority of our citizens cannot be trusted to walk through a field without destroying or attacking its crops and stock. But respect for the environment can no more be brought by denying access to it, than swimming can be taught on the edge of the pool. Third, conflicts between access users would be reduced, as walkers would have more space to enjoy and would be less jealous in their attitudes towards it. A countryside over which we can wander freely, in which we are trusted to act responsibly and with sensitivity, will also be a countryside in which the varying, specialised pursuits of minorities can far more easily be found a place. Common access will serve to establish the decency of the majority as a visible fact, thus opening the way to tolerance of non-pedestrian uses. Such users themselves will have a real stake in the entire countryside and consequently a greater respect for it and their fellow users.

WHAT WE NEED

• The Right of Common Access: This right will allow all to wander freely in the countryside, subject to certain restrictions. You must do no damage—to crops, gates, fences, buildings and so forth. You must take care not to injure or kill farm stock—which means keeping dogs on a lead or under close control—and special care must be taken, especially during the spring, not to disturb birds and other animals. You must respect the privacy of those who live in the countryside. Though you will be able to walk over the property of both public and private landowners, you must avoid gardens, or the land immediately adjacent to where people live. The presumption is thus one of general access but at all times visitors must keep off growing crops.

Landowners, for their part, must keep paths clear of growing crops. They will not be able to erect signs like 'Keep Out' or 'Trespassers Will Be Prosecuted' (they won't be), unless authorised to do so by their local authority. This right of common access will apply only to those on foot. Motor traffic, of whatever sort, will be prohibited from using open country or farmland except where special provision is made for it.

- The Land Bank: Later we shall be arguing for the creation of a Land Bank, which would comprise some ten per cent of the countryside. Land would be taken out of agriculture and commercial forestry, and given over to other uses, including public recreation. It will be up to the county and regional councils to meet the recreational needs of their areas, and the Land Bank will complement existing national and country parks. Some of the areas within the Land Bank put aside for recreation might be quite small. Others, like Sherwood Forest, whose future we discuss later, could be very large.

We would also like inner-city boroughs to be given the opportunity of participating in planning the use of recreational facilities in nearby rural counties. For example, Islington and Hackney should have some say in what happens to the Land Bank in Essex, Southwark's needs should influence what happens in Kent, and the people of Notting Hill must be involved in the determination of the recreational policies of the Chilterns.

- Better Public Transport: The Countryside Commission, in its 1984 survey, asked the simple question: Are you happy about the amount you visit the countryside? Forty-two per cent said they were. The rest said they weren't: they wanted to go more often. And it comes as no surprise that only 3 per cent of social class A don't go to the countryside and 60 per cent go a lot, whereas 25 per cent of social class F never go, and only 25 per cent go frequently. The unemployed, needless to say, spend even less time out of their towns. It may be that some of those at the bottom of the social heap wouldn't go to the countryside even if they had the means, but many would, and it is vital that cheap public transport is available for them to do so. To this end, we advocate the establishment of a public transport fund, collected from central government and administered by county councils, which will provide cheap transport with the express aim of enabling people to get out of the cities and into the countryside. It should be free to all those who are out of work.

Markerstone on Old Drove Road, from Harlech to London

Aberedw Hill, near Builth Wells

The Ridgeway and Uffington Castle, Berkshire

Barbary Castle Clump, Wiltshire

Marshland, Romney Marsh

Priory Woods, Kent

Forestry Commission Picnic Place, Forest of Dean

Sunrise, Forest of Dean

Smallholding, Forest of Dean

Sheep, Romney Marsh

Rye Cattle Market

Ducks on Small Farm, East Sussex

Pig in Cider Orchard, Forest of Dean

Smallholding, East Sussex

Smallholding, East Sussex

Smallholding, East Sussex

Smallholding, East Sussex

Forestry Commission Land, Forest of Dean

Industrial Heritage, Forest of Dean

Hung Rabbit, Wiltshire

Stubble Burning, East Kent

Kemsley Paper Mills from the Swale

Edge of Murston Nature Reserve, East Kent

Dying Trees, Northumberland

CHAPTER FIVE

A New Deal
for the Land

A New Deal
for the Land

SINCE THE Second World War rural Britain has been transformed by a process often called the 'second agricultural revolution'. Farming has been organised around the principle of profit since the eighteenth century, and it had for long been disciplined by the exigencies of the market. But over the last four decades a transformation in the technology of food production, accompanied by a system of state support, has enabled farmers to adopt practices undreamed of earlier this century. The mechanisation of agriculture has made much of the work force redundant. Advances in genetics have produced unprecedented increases in output from both animals and crops. Farm animals have been removed from the fields for some or all of their lives, and over much of the country farms have become bigger, more dependent on large inputs of capital and more specialised. Agricultural entrepreneurship has followed precepts of rationalisation formerly apparent only in other industries, and any sense of technological continuity has been shattered within the lifetime of most of today's farmers.

It is worth making clear at the outset that the second agricultural revolution cannot be explained away by simply invoking technological determinism. Nor do the economic demands of contemporary agriculture owe much to the workings of a free market. Individual farmers may act as if they are governed by market rationality, but over the last forty years the state has intervened decisively and continuously as the midwife of technological change and the guarantor of profitability. The 1947 Agriculture Act offered the single-minded pursuit, under the direction of the Ministry of Agriculture, of efficiency and stability, while other departments, both locally and nationally, were left to mop up the social consequences among those who suffered by this policy, and to fight a rearguard action to halt the environmental despoliation which accompanied it. The technological transformation of British agriculture has not been a product of the 'hidden hand' of the market, but the result of policy, consciously pursued and publicly encouraged up to the present day.

The forty-year period of agricultural expansion is coming to an end. The EEC's Common Agricultural Policy (CAP) is now costing the community over £12 billion a year. It is not money well spent. The CAP has made a few farmers rich, bankrupted many smaller ones and made the family food-bill higher than it need be. Pressure for its reform comes from many quarters: from consumer organisations, from big food-chains like Tesco, from conservationists, from economists, and from many farmers. In its place we must construct a policy which will ensure that food production takes account of the nation's health and all the other needs of the countryside.

It is only within the last year or two that the farming lobby has ceased to tell us that we must produce more food and that this is the way to a solvent and prosperous agriculture, which is itself the key to a healthy and beautiful countryside. The lobby no longer believes this. The Minister of Agriculture no longer believes it. But one may reasonably wonder how many individual farmers and landowners believe it. We suspect that most are hoping that the current pressures against over-production and the apparent reluctance of the government and tax-payers to finance it are but a passing phase. Certainly the reaction of most farmers and owners to any restrictions on output, whether by quota, set-aside or lower prices, will be to think how they can avoid the economic ill-effects thereof; and that is not a calculation in which care for the environment or the interests of others in the countryside are likely to figure significantly. The farming industry, at any rate those whom it has permitted to speak for it, has happily accepted a policy which has caused immense environmental destruction, closed off statutory rights of access, channelled money from the poor to the rich and led to the costly dumping of food on markets where it does appalling damage to Third World producers.

Whatever else is in doubt, it is clear that the farming and landowning lobby and the Ministry of Agriculture cannot be allowed to write the new programme. That must be done for them.

THE NATIONAL HEALTH

One of the most remarkable aspects of British and EEC agricultural policy is that it takes absolutely no account of diet. Yet malnutrition, associated with eating too much of the wrong things and not enough of the right, is a major European (and American) killer. The government has reacted to recent reports which highlight the relationship between poor diet and illness with a shameful lack of urgency.

Since 1983 two major reports on the relationship between diet and health have appeared. The National Advisory Committee on Nutrition Education (which has the unfortunate acronym NACNE) was set up under the chairmanship of Professor Philip James in 1979. Its first report, produced in 1981, was suppressed by the Department of Health. Further reports were drafted in 1982 and 1983, and their findings have been generally endorsed by the medical profession and by the government's Committee on Medical Aspects of Food Policy (whose intriguing acronym is COMA).

Over a third of all adults in Britain are overweight. The culprits: fat and sugar. The death rates from coronary heart diseases in the UK are among the highest of anywhere in the world. Again, excess consumption of fats and sugar has much to do with it. They also contribute, when combined with a lack of dietary fibre, to the high incidence of both diabetes and gall-bladder disease. Cancers of the large bowel and the colon, as well as diverticular disease, are attributed by the NACNE report to an insufficient intake of fibre; and too much fat and salt increase the incidence of strokes. In short, many of the major diseases of today are a direct consequence of eating too much fat, sugar and salt, and too little fibre. Over one hundred and seventy thousand people die of heart disease in Britain every year; over seventy thousand people are afflicted by strokes; and over ten thousand people die of bowel and colon cancers. The NACNE report called for reductions of fat in our diet from 40 per cent to 30-5 per cent of our total energy intake, and it recommended that sugar intake be cut from the average 38kg per person a year to 20kg. In 1981 the average amount of salt in our diet was 7-10 g a day. In the long term, the committee recommended that salt consumption should be reduced to 3g a day. As far as fibre was concerned, the committee wished to see our daily intake rise from 20g to 30g.

So far the government's reactions to the NACNE and COMA reports have been pitiful. Its supporters might argue that recently introduced proposals for the nutritional labelling of some foods are proof of its concern for better health education—but these do not go nearly far enough. Most foods will now be statutorily labelled to show their fat content; but we should also be able to find out at a glance how much sugar and salt is contained in what we buy. Many countries already require by law that foodstuffs should list fat, sugar and salt content. This country must as well.

The boom in 'health foods' has convinced many people in the food industry that consumers are concerned not only about what they eat, in terms of dietary balance, but with the quality of the produce they buy. Many people are quite happy to pay the small premium for free-range eggs, and for cereal products which haven't been dosed in pesticides and fertilizers. Meanwhile, 'real meat', which comes from animals which are humanely reared (and often fed on organic and additive-free foodstuffs) is becoming more widely available. All this is to be encouraged.

Nutritional labelling is vitally important, but the government has an equally important role to play in ensuring that farmers don't overproduce food of which we should be eating less. Over the last decade both the EEC and our own governments have connived with the retail industry to make the public eat more of what we should be eating less of. Witness the aggressive advertising campaigns encouraging us to eat high-fat butter rather than low-fat margarines. Even more disgraceful was the Commission's attempt to reduce the over-production of dairy products by trying to raise the fat content of milk and thus slice the top off the butter mountain. And Britain's individual reaction to the butter surplus was similarly irresponsible: the cut-price Christmas butter scheme helped to offload some forty thousand tons of surplus—or, put more bluntly, it encouraged people, especially the poor and old, whose diets are in any case less than ideal, to harm their health.

Dairy products contribute around a third of our dietary fat intake, and meat products about a quarter. Yet very lean carcasses are excluded from the price support schemes. Indeed, intensive methods of meat production encourage animals to lay down fat rather than lean meat. The farming lobby has persistently argued that surplus production could be reduced if the public consumed more of whatever product is in question, whereas the real need is for farmers to lower production to match declining trends in consumption, and to produce dairy and meat products with lower fat contents. (The Milk Marketing Board argued against the milk quota scheme which the EEC introduced in 1984. It believed that better marketing would solve the problem of surplus production, because it would encourage consumers to buy more milk, cheese, butter and so forth. Put another way, it wished to offload costs onto the National Health Service.)

It is quite clear that existing trends in consumption already presage a new pattern in farming (assuming that supply is brought in line with demand). Consumption of butter and eggs has been falling for many years, and many people are now eating less red meat and more white meat. (Poultry is much less fatty than other meats, and chicken consumption in Britain rose by 120 per cent in the thirty years after 1950). Not long ago to be a vegetarian was to be a freak, and hefty meat-eating was considered a prerequisite of longevity. Indeed, Lord Byron surmised that two of Shelley's children died young because he had raised them on a vegetarian diet. But attitudes have changed, as has our knowledge of dietary needs, and many now extol the non-carnivorous way of life. Increasing numbers concur with Shelley that vegetarianism strikes 'at the root of all evil', and there are now well over a million vegetarians in Britain and a further million who do not eat red meat. By the end of this century we shall be eating less meat, fewer dairy products, and more vegetables, pulses and fresh fruit.

All this will have repercussions on how we farm. In particular we shall see dramatic declines in the numbers of pigs and cows. And land presently used to grow cereals for animal fodder will be put to other uses. We shall be using less fertiliser and pesticide, and the grazing of cattle will have to be practised more extensively. The abolition of intensive pig- and poultry-rearing will also mean that these animals will be

kept outdoors, and land currently growing cereals for feed
will be returned to pasture.

TOO MUCH OF A BAD THING

In the 1930s, Britain was only 30 per cent self-sufficient
in food which could be grown here. Rapid growth after the
war ensured that self-sufficiency rose to 62 per cent by the
time we joined the EEC in 1973, and by 1984 we were 78 per
cent self-sufficient in temperate food products. Britain is now
virtually self-sufficient in eggs and potatoes, and an over-
producer of cereals. The EEC as a whole over-produces beef,
poultry, pig-meat, sugar, dairy-produce and cereals. The
House of Lords Select Committee on the European
Communities *(Farm Price Proposals, 1984-85)* calculated that
if the current policies remained unchanged, milk production
in the EEC would exceed demand by 40 per cent by 1990, and
the demand for cereals by 1990 "could be in the order of one
hundred and fourteen million tonnes, while production could
reach about one hundred and thirty-seven million
tonnes".

The storage and disposal of these surpluses is
enormously costly. Under the present system EEC agencies
buy the farmers' produce when the market price falls below
the minimum guaranteed price set each year by the farm
ministers. If the market price returns to the guaranteed
minimum, the produce is gradually put on the market. If it
doesn't, it must be sold at a loss or retained in storage. The
cost of storing surpluses takes up an ever-increasing
proportion of the CAP budget—the cost of storage in 1987 is
likely to reach a staggering 25 per cent or more of the total
CAP budget. Even more is spent on subsidising exports.
(Many food stuffs can only be exported if the EEC pays a
subsidy which makes the world-market price up to the
guaranteed price.) The EEC also operates a policy of

'community preference', whereby imports from countries outside the EEC are taxed to ensure that they cannot undercut EEC prices. Not surprisingly, the USA, desperately seeking markets for its vast agricultural surpluses, has recently and rightly accused the EEC of operating the world's best organised protection racket and is now beginning to retaliate.

Some products are particularly heavily subsidised. In 1983 the EEC paid out more than £100 per cow, and the economist Paul Cheshire has pointed out that British dairy production probably has the effect of actually reducing our gross national product. Such was the drain on resources caused by over-production of milk that in 1984 the EEC was forced to introduce a system of quotas to curb production, and in Britain £50 million was put aside to pay farmers to give up dairying. Farmers were understandably furious. Successive governments had for years been encouraging them to raise output. Now they were being told to cut it. The milk quotas are just a taste of things to come, and it has only been the wrecking tactics of West Germany's farm minister that have prevented the EEC dramatically reducing support prices for cereals in recent years. The reprieve for the cereal farmers will only be temporary, and in the coming years a mixture of price cuts and quotas will inevitably be forced on both cereal and beef producers.

According to the Think Tank paper on 'Reducing Agricultural Subsidies', produced by a group of experts in the Cabinet Office, the British tax-payer is subsidising British farmers to the tune of £20,000 every year. To make things worse, CAP policies have also added to the price of our food bill. Obviously, this is particularly hard on those with low incomes and those without work. In 1980 the Institute for Fiscal Studies calculated that UK consumers were paying £2.8 billion more for their food as a result of restriction and quotas placed on foreign imports, and in 1985 Tesco submitted a paper to the House of Lords in which it suggested that the CAP added between £75 and £184 a year to the average family food bill. It concluded its report on the CAP with the comment: "When all the Community governments are concerned to contain inflation these, surely, are the economics of madness". Quite so.

Another shameful aspect of the protective policies adopted by the EEC has been their effect on poor countries. Let us take, as an example, the production of sugar. The EEC pays out around £475 for every hectare of sugar beet grown. High levels of support and the colossally high quotas allowed to our farmers meant that between 1973 and 1983 EEC sugar production rose by 46 per cent. The EEC was thus producing one and a half times more sugar than it needed, and in 1983 it was costing £2 million a day to dump the surplus on the world market, where prices were considerably lower. At one time Europe imported nearly all its sugar from abroad, particularly from Jamaica, Guyana, Brazil and the Caribbean. Under the Lomé Convention, the EEC has agreed to continue importing some sugar from African, Caribbean and Pacific countries at EEC prices, but our dumping policies have reduced the price of sugar on the world market to such a low level that it doesn't cover the cost of production even in those countries which are the lowest-cost producers. Here is Sir Richard Body, a Conservative MP, on the effects which our policies are having: "If one takes Guyana, the cost of producing sugar there is about £140 a tonne. [But] it has to sell sugar at the world market price of £85 a tonne. So there's a country which is almost entirely dependent on sugar for all its foreign exchange, and yet the export has to be put on the world market at a very terrible loss... This is causing great poverty in Guyana". (Quoted from *Agriculture, The Triumph and the Shame*, London, 1982.)

INTENSIFICATION AND SPECIALISATION: THE ROAD TO RUIN?

Agriculture is a high-tech industry, and there is no reason to suppose that the technological revolution affecting crop varieties, fertiliser deployment, waste disposal and machinery design won't continue to influence the way we farm. Many of the large farmers plan their farming on computers, seldom get on a tractor, and use whatever technology is available to maximise their profits. Oliver Walston, farmer and TV presenter, has seen changes on his big farm in Cambridgeshire that have occurred over much of lowland England: "We're completely dependent on fertilisers and insecticides and fungicides. Until the war this wasn't the case at all. The fertility on this farm, up until 1939, all came out of the back end of an animal—in other words, it came from manure. Nowadays, animals play very little part in farms in this area, and fertility comes out of plastic bags— rock phosphate from Morocco, nitrogen and potash from England. We use a lot of very big machines, too. Just to give you some idea, there's a photograph outside this office which shows about eighty-five people sitting around a table having a harvest celebration supper in 1946. In those days we farmed about six hundred hectares and we needed eighty-five people. Today in 1985 we're farming double the area, twelve hundred hectares, and we need twelve people." Walston has twenty tractors, three lorries, four air-conditioned combine harvesters and two sprayers which can spray a hectare in a couple of minutes.

One of the most tragic aspects of modern farming policy has been its disregard for farm-workers and for the small farmers. Not that the loss of farm-workers and the small farmer is a new phenomenon. Labour has been leaving the land for at least two centuries. William Cobbett was already bemoaning the loss of the small farmer in the 1830s. In one parish which he visited on his *Rural Rides* he found that one farmer held by lease, as one farm, "the lands that men, now living, can remember to have formed fourteen farms, bringing up in a respectable way, fourteen families". In 1939 Lord Addison, a former Minister of Agriculture, reflected on the continuing exodus: "The number of those employed on the land (whole-time and part-time) has been declining all these years, but it has diminished by more than one hundred thousand since 1930. The total in Great Britain has fallen by nearly three hundred thousand since 1891. Since the beginning of the present century nearly a quarter of a million workers have quietly drifted from the country to the town, and this whilst for many of the self-same years the chances of employment in the towns were worse than we have any previous record of". Addison proposed policies which might have stemmed the loss. But no one in power took any notice, as statistics for the last forty years show. The farm labour force has been reduced by two-thirds since the last war, and UK agriculture now provides employment for less than three per cent of the civil work force (compared to an average 8 per cent for the EEC as a whole). Since 1973 the number of hired agricultural workers has fallen by 20 per cent. During the same period the number of unemployed has risen from 3.1 per cent of the potentially employable population to over 12 per cent. That the farm labour force should continue to decline, and that we should persist with policies which ensure that it does, is quite scandalous, especially at this time of growing unemployment.

The increasingly capital-intensive nature of British farming has drawn farmers into the embrace of a wide complex of industrial companies involved in the marketing, distribution and retailing of food. Agriculture is slowly being incorporated into sectors of the engineering, chemical and food-processing industries; in other words into agribusiness, whose rise implies not only the rationalisation of farming, but the growth of a food-production system away from the land. The agribusiness conglomerates are actively involved in changing dietary habits and restructuring the farming industry and food-marketing. They wield enormous power, yet remain largely impervious to control by politicians and consumers. In Britain few agribusiness companies have attempted to restructure agriculture by farming themselves. Instead, and just as efficiently, they have worked by proxy, seeking out highly market-orientated farmers with whom to place contracts. They have thus avoided both the high cost of land purchase and the cost of buying managerial expertise to run food-producing enterprises. However, agribusinesses have been crucial in accelerating trends towards speciali-sation and the concentration of production onto fewer and larger farms. While the large farmers, particularly in the eastern lowlands, are sucked relentlessly along the path of 'industrial logic', the small ones play an ever more marginal role in British food production. We can now discern a dual farming economy in which the bulk of production happens on a few capital-intensive farms, leaving a much larger number to concentrate on those sectors of production which, for one reason or another, agribusiness has yet to penetrate. Governments have done nothing to counteract this trend. Indeed, they have reinforced it by ploughing money into the industrialised sector and doing little for the small and part-time farmer.

Over much of the country the mixed farm has gone. Farm animals, whose manure was once needed to keep the land fertile, have been banished into factory units, and many farms in south and east England are devoted entirely to arable cropping, while stock-rearing and dairying have shifted westward. The introduction of herbicides after the last war meant that farmers could grow the same crop on the same field year after year, thus abandoning rotation and the use of stock. This specialisation was encouraged by MAFF propaganda and by the support system, which, on good land, tended to favour the production of arable crops over stock rearing. In order to get the best returns on capital, many farmers have forsaken diversity for monoculture. The outcome, as the economists J.K. Bowers and Paul Cheshire have noted, "is that economies of joint production have been sacrificed for the dubious economies of specialisation". (*Agriculture, The Countryside and Land Use.* London, 1983)

Forty years ago nothing on the farm was wasted. Manure was returned to the land and straw was used as bedding or fodder. Today, Britain's farmers burn six million tonnes of straw every year—about half the annual crop. And two-thirds of the manure and slurry produced by our livestock are wasted, with less than a third of the country's crops and grass receiving any at all. Distorted markets, favouring arable cropping over livestock production, the relative cheapness of artificial fertilisers and their ease of application, the widespread use of pesticides and the throw-away ethos encouraged by MAFF have led farmers to behave as they do.

This cannot be allowed to continue. First, because it sterilises the countryside and poses unacceptable risks to workers, residents and visitors to the countryside. Second, because food produced in this way is increasingly unacceptable to the consumer.

The intensive livestock sector has also run into trouble over recent years. Bought-in feed now accounts for two-thirds of costs in the poultry and pig-meat sector, and the high price of cereals has made many businesses unprofitable. The industry has steadfastly maintained that in real terms factory farming has reduced the price of pig-meat and poultry. On welfare grounds alone, the intensive rearing of farm animals must be abolished. In practice this will be all for the good of the farmer. Recent studies have shown that returns on free-range pigs can be just as good as those on intensively reared animals, and it will help the industry to re-integrate livestock and arable production. In the long term, the mixed farm, where 'corn and horn' complement one another, is the most efficient system, and the one least damaging to the ecology of the soil. The mixed farmers will return all manure to the land, they will rotate their crops, they will use straw, and they will grow some of the feed required for their stock. Their fertiliser and pesticide bills will be lower than those of the specialist arable farmers, and they will be better able to survive the vagaries of the market. If one crop has a run of bad years they will not go out of business, which may well be the fate of the specialists.

A RESCUE PLAN

Agriculture provides us with one of the clearest examples of 'jobless growth': massive increases in production have been accompanied by a massive decline in employment. "There were thirty of us here in 1970," said one Yorkshire tractor-driver. "Now there's only eight of us left. I don't like it. But it's progress, isn't it?" Here the word 'progress' is used as an excuse for something—in this case, the loss of labour from the land—which is considered undesirable but unavoidable. Underlying the farm-worker's observation is the belief that all the fancy technology available to today's farmer, being available, must be used. If the new technologies are beckoning us down a certain path, then we must follow it, even to a dead end.

If we fail to challenge this view of progress, we accept that the destiny of the countryside lies beyond our control. And if the Government continues to do what Galbraith called "running the economy without the intervention of human intelligence" (a pretty good description of our present agricultural policy), then production will become concentrated on fewer and larger farms; the workforce will diminish year by year; and eventually we will be left with a monotonous, unpeopled landscape—not the "fair field full of folk" we want.

Our measure of progress is the antithesis of the yardstick

commonly used by the leaders of the agricultural industry to justify the changes of the past seventy or so years. "Progress", wrote Herbert Read, who began and ended his life on a Yorkshire farm, "is measured by the degree of differentiation within a society. If the individual is a unit in a corporate mass, his life will be limited, dull and mechanical...Progress is measured by richness and intensity of experience". Progress for some of us implies, in the interests of both social justice and efficient agriculture, that the private ownership of land should be abolished. Lord Addison, just before the last war, said that "The case for the national acquisition of land is unassailable and widely admitted". Yet since that time even the Labour Party has steered well clear of the subject, save to suggest that tenanted land should be taken into public ownership. Public ownership of all land seems to be a millennialist solution; the respect for property ownership in this country is simply too powerful an emotion to be overturned in any reasonable time-span.

During the last hundred years we have witnessed two significant changes in land ownership. First, the number of holdings has declined, and it continues to do so. And the number of tenanted holdings has steadily fallen, while owner-occupation has experienced a corresponding rise. In 1891 there were four hundred and seventy two thousand holdings in England and Wales. Of these only sixty nine thousand were owner-occupied. In 1974 the number of holdings had fallen to two hundred and nine thousand, one hundred and twenty-nine thousand of which were owner-occupied. Over half the land area is now farmed by owners. During the decade up to 1982, 40 per cent of holdings under two hectares, 23 per cent of holdings between two and 20 hectares, and 15 per cent of those between 20 and 40 hectares were lost, and every year the number of available tenancies becomes less. In 1981 only 11 per cent of the tenanted land which fell vacant was relet. The rest was taken in hand by the owners or sold. Recent legislation, which aimed to encourage landowners to let more farms, doesn't appear to be affecting this trend significantly. At the same time, the amount of land held under the county council smallholdings scheme has been falling. This is particularly sad as the scheme is intended to help young men and women onto the first rung of the farming ladder. It has now become all but impossible for those who don't stand to inherit land (either as tenants or owners) to get into farming. The tenancies are not available, and land prices preclude all but the richest from buying their way in.

Public ownership of land does not always mean that it will be used in the best interests of the community. Eastern Europe is evidence of that. Conversely, there are plenty of examples proving that state ownership in democratic countries, albeit in an atmosphere of continuous argument, can work—look, for example, at the situation in large parts of Switzerland, Australia and the USA. Nor does the private ownership of land necessarily mean that it is managed to the benefit of one person and to the detriment of the rest of us. Both good and bad landlords preside over both big and small estates in this country. What we require in the immediate future is not total state ownership of land—though public ownership has its place—but the nationalisation of some of the owners' property rights. This can be achieved by a mix of fiscal incentives, planning controls and taxation devices, and over the following pages we deal with these. In addition, we advocate the following measures which will have a direct and immediate effect on the pattern of landownership:

• There should be a freeze on all tenancies. When a tenancy falls vacant, it must be relet. If a landlord does not wish to re-let, he must offer it for sale to the county council (or the regional council in Scotland).

• It is tempting to suggest that there should be a ceiling on how much land one family can farm. However, the obstacles to such a reform would be almost insuperable. Landowners could avoid it by setting up new companies, and those who complied might react by shedding awkward and unmanageable parcels of land. As price support is reduced, and production grants abolished, we shall see land prices fall. Many landowners will be obliged to sell off their land (which must first be offered to public bodies), and a tightening of capital transfer tax laws will ensure that over a very short period of time the great estates will be broken down into smaller units.

FINANCIAL REFORMS

Many of the reforms we wish to see could be promoted by simple changes in pricing policy. At present, the high support prices for cereals and many other products have led to high land prices. These in turn have encouraged farmers to be more exploitative. Grazing marshes have been ploughed up; fertilisers have been poured onto the soil in ever-increasing quantities; and land which formerly supported low input—low output systems of farming has been switched to intensive use.

• Abolishing Export Subsidies. The House of Lords Select Committee on the European Communities (1982-3 Farm Price Settlement) suggested, very sensibly, that excess production should be sold competitively on the world market free of subsidy. We agree. Export subsidies should be phased out over a four-year period.

• Reducing Price Support. The aim of CAP should be to achieve a reasonable degree of self-sufficiency without raising prices more than 10 per cent above world-market levels. With the fall in prices, production of such commodities as wheat, milk, barley, sugar, oil-seed rape and beef would be reduced. This would be accompanied by a drop in land prices and the reversion of much arable land to grass, thus liberating land for the free-ranging of pigs and poultry and for other agricultural and non-agricultural purposes. If price-support expenditure were halved, then the UK would save around £700 million a year. These measures would be appreciated both by the tax-payer and consumer and by trading partners outside the EEC. For example, we would see a dramatic fall in the amount of sugar-beet grown here, an end to dumping, and the establishment of a world price which would benefit those countries where sugar is—or was—the mainstay of their economy. The lowering of import taxes would also benefit other cereal producers.

• Production grants must be phased out. There should be an immediate halt to all drainage—conversion grants, and the headage-payment system which applies to sheep and beef production in the less favoured areas (covering about half of Britain), and other headage payments such as the annual ewe premium and the beef variable premium, should be replaced by a system of direct income-support to those farmers who need it. A scheme of Land Management Payments should be available to those farmers who agree to abide by the management, conservation and access agreements which will be drawn up between farmers and county councils, whose responsibility it will be to administer grants and determine local land-use policy.

ENCOURAGING MIXED FARMING

We wish to see a reversion to mixed systems of farming which are less reliant on heavy inputs. The first priority is to wean farmers off chemicals, as far as is practicably possible. We have argued that the present amounts of fertilisers and pesticides are bad for the soil, bad for nature conservation and dangerous to our health. The Think Tank on 'Reducing

Agricultural Subsidies' suggested that a modest 15 per cent tax on fertilisers and pesticides would help to discourage excessive use. Such a tax would yield between £75 and £100 million a year, money which could be used to help farmers to switch from high-input to low-input systems of farming and to revert from specialist cropping to mixed crop and stock farming. County councils and water authorities should have the power to curb the use of fertilisers and this should lead to considerable reductions in their use. Many specialist cereal farmers would wish to take on stock and re-establish rotations in order to maintain soil fertility without having to use large quantities of bag fertiliser. Changes in the price-support system and stringent laws on pesticide use will also favour the mixed farmer.

We also wish to see the price-support system reward the farmer for quality. It should discourage the production of low-quality feed grain and provide a premium for those farmers who produce food with low inputs of chemicals or organically. Price support for beef and poultry should be higher for those farmers who rear their animals on unfertilised grass extensively, than for those who keep them indoors. Other measures such as the abolition of intensive livestock units, and the introduction of a premium for lean-meat producers will further encourage farmers to move towards mixed systems.

HEALTHY FOOD

All food should be labelled to show what fat, sugar and salt it contains. It looks as if we will get labelling for fat by 1988 or 1989 and other schemes are in train, but we still need much more information than these schemes will provide. All meat should be labelled to show where it was raised and how, whether it was reared on artificial feed or grass, indoors or outdoors and so on. Cereal products and vegetables should carry labels stating whether fertilisers and pesticides were used in their production. And price support should reflect the relative dangers of eating certain foodstuffs. Low fat brands of margarine are better for health than butter, and the consumer subsidy on butter should be abolished: it makes no sense. At the same time, and for the same reasons, the fat content of milk should be reduced to 2 per cent from the present average of well over 3 per cent.

There is also an urgent need for a public health campaign. We already have laws which oblige tobacco manufacturers to include health warnings on their advertisements and products. There are strong arguments for extending this system to the food industry, particularly for meat and dairy products. There would be no point in entrusting responsibilities for health campaigns to MAFF, which is still producing fatuous advice on such topics as 'The Right Way To Use Canned Foods' ("We are all familiar with canned foods... However, it is easy to take them for granted, and like all other foods it is important to use them with common sense..."). The Department of Health and Social Security must take on the campaign to convince people that to live long one must watch what one eats.

THE LAND BANK

Food production can be reduced in a number of ways. A system of quotas can be used, as now happens in the dairy industry. But quotas, though effective, are crude; and they may have unpleasant environmental and social side effects. Dairy farmers, who had been encouraged to expand their production in past years, were locked into a lengthy production cycle and were faced with an immediate loss of income which many could not sustain. Since dairying is one of the major undertakings of the family-farm sector, the introduction of milk quotas sat rather oddly with the ostensible social objectives of the CAP to support viable rural populations, especially in LFAs. The dairy farmers in areas like Dyfed have been particularly badly hit.

Production can also be reduced by lowering support prices, which in many areas will have the effect of reducing the amount of food produced per hectare and pushing farmers onto the low-input—low-output road. Or production can be reduced by taking land out of agricultural use. We advocate a mix of these strategies.

Britain should establish a Land Bank. We suggest that by the end of this century ten per cent of all land should be taken out of agricultural production, and a further five per cent shifted from private to public ownership and retained for farming. Much of the ten per cent would become publicly owned and all would be used for non-agricultural purposes—conservation, deciduous forestry, recreation and so on. The other five per cent taken into public ownership would continue to be farmed, but it would be broken up into smallholdings.

There has been much initial scepticism within the farming industry at the idea of taking land out of production, but now even officials within the Ministry of Agriculture accept that such a programme will be needed. Estimates of the amount of agricultural land that would need to come out of production in the UK now in order to stop surplus production extends up to three million hectares, and in 1987 it was suggested that between 4.5 and 6 million hectares of agricultural land would need to be taken out of production over the next thirty years.

It is therefore clear that even if production is restricted by controls on inputs, there will be no difficulty in releasing ten per cent of farmed land into the Land Bank. Some counties might take more, some less. It will be up to the county councils in England and Wales, and the regional councils in Scotland, to decide exactly which areas should be taken into the Land Bank. They will vary from small patches of grassland to vast tracts of moorland, heath and estuarine cropland. It will also be the responsibility of the (democratically elected) councils to decide what uses this land should be put to. Some would go for recreation. Around urban areas these blocks would complement the country parks which already exist, and they could be managed in similar ways. In the uplands, they might be grouse moors from which shooting has been banned. Much of the Land Bank would have conservation as its first object.

In particular, we believe that all land which depends on continuous capital inputs for farming should be set aside. For example, keeping many lowland areas in cereal production behind the sea-walls of East Anglia is very costly. The solution is simple: abandon arable farming and break down the sea-walls. This would create marvellous areas of marshland which would soon become as rich in wildfowl as the nature reserves at Minsmere and Titchwell Marsh. We believe that many farmers would be happy to see their farms join the Land Bank and come out of agricultural production, and to be paid by the councils to manage their farms for the purposes of conservation and recreation. Those farmers who don't wish to join the Land Bank scheme, but whose land is designated for it, would be bought out by public bodies.

The government has already been forced into a tentative experiment with payments to farmers for such purposes in Environmentally Sensitive Areas (ESAs). But these are a makeshift and ad hoc response to immediate pressures. They are vitiated by the small area covered, the low level of payments to farmers involved, the minimal standards which farmers must meet in them, and the lack of any real planning for wildlife and access.

We have suggested that five per cent of British farmland should be brought into public ownership and remain as farmland. This will not be part of the Land Bank, but we include it here because the management of both will be determined by the local community. The county and regional councils will determine policies for the Land Bank, which owners and managers will put into practice, and they will also be the landlords of the five per cent. As landlords, they will not only be able to determine the size of holdings, but the way in which they are farmed. Their main objective will be a social one: to enable the greatest possible number of people to make a living off the land. Tenants will be expected to farm efficiently and decently. They will be encouraged to produce high-quality food and to use the minimum of inputs. On well-drained land this may involve the free-ranging of pigs or poultry. On low-fertility grassland, the maintenance of suckler herds will be favoured along with sheep fattening. In some instances the county councils will establish co-operatives which will help to increase the efficiency of individual farms by enabling them to share resources such as machinery. Where upland and lowland farms are in close proximity, deals may be made which allow the upland farmer to overwinter his sheep in the lowlands. In Great Britain, the total area under arable crops and temporary grass comes to seven million hectares. If five per cent of this were brought into public ownership, the county and regional councils would become landlords over three hundred and fifty thousand hectares. Let us suppose that the average size of their smallholdings on this land will be twenty hectares. The number of tenancies created would be in the order of eighteen thousand.

TAKING THE CRUELTY OUT OF FARMING

We turn now to domestic animals. We can confidently predict that we shall progressively consume less meat and smaller quantities of dairy produce over the coming years. Indeed, the decline in consumption has been apparent for some time. Some people have foresaken meat for health reasons—fat can be a killer; others because they cannot afford it—the Sunday joint is a thing of the past for many families; and still others because they find modern methods of livestock husbandry repugnant. A National Opinion Poll Survey in 1983 found that 88 per cent of those questioned favoured reforms of factory farming; 90 per cent wanted laws which would give farm animals the freedom to turn round, groom themselves and stretch, freedom presently denied to millions of animals; 75 per cent wanted a ban on the live export of farm animals; and a slightly higher percentage wanted to see a ban on the ritual slaughter of animals. Two years earlier the House of Commons had reported on 'Animal Welfare in Poultry, Pig and Veal Calf Production'. It had called for a ban on the rearing of crated veal, the phasing out of close-confinement stalls for pregnant sows and batteries for hens. The government accepted the report's suggestions 'in principle'. Apart from moving to abolish veal crates, it ignored them. The reforms which we list below will put an end to cruel systems of farming, and any government with the slightest concern for animal welfare will adopt them immediately.

We wish to see the following practices banned:

- The import of veal reared in crates.
- The confinement of pregnant sows in stalls.
- The use of battery hen-cages. Hens should either be free-ranged, or kept in buildings which allow them ample freedom of movement and access to grazing plots outdoors.
- The ritual slaughter of any animal.
- The export of any live farm animal. As the Farm Animal Welfare Co-ordinating Committee commented: "Virtually every unofficial, unheralded investigation [of live export] reveals conditions of hardship, suffering and undue stress".
- The import of any animals—dead or alive—which have been reared under methods banned in this country.

RICH WORLD, POOR WORLD

The obsession with self-sufficiency has underpinned the expansionist policies which have led us into the present mess. That this country, and others in Europe, should have striven to increase output after the Second World War was quite reasonable. After all, we were dependent on foreign countries for well over half our food supplies and the war had imperilled them. But, if the world became embroiled in another war, we shouldn't be worrying about U-boat blockades. As Sir Herman Bondi, formerly chief scientist to MAFF, has pointed out, nuclear war would disrupt or halt the distribution and availability of fossil fuels, electricity and water, three inputs without which today's high-tech agriculture could not function, even for a few days. Even if the war was non-nuclear, attacks on power stations, fertiliser factories and roads would cause havoc, "reducing production by perhaps four-fifths", according to Bondi. Modern agriculture, having displaced labour with capital and low-input systems with high-input systems, has made mass starvation an inevitable consequence of future war, not the reverse, as was intended. There is much to be said for avoiding over-dependence on foreign supplies, maintaining employment on the land, and keeping down import bills. But there is no justification for producing permanent surpluses which distort the world market.

An Oxfam study of food, power and poverty— *Cultivating Hunger* (Oxford, 1984)—concluded that "something has gone terribly wrong with our world food system. More than enough food is being produced to feed the entire population of the planet, but the food is increasingly out of the reach of the poor. The current emphasis on increasing food production is no solution; it's not food that is in short supply, but simple justice. World food supplies are at record high levels. But the food is being grown in the wrong place, and at a price that the world's poor cannot afford".

The solutions to these problems are not simple; for each commodity there is likely to be a complex set of trade-offs, involving both economic and environmental benefits and disbenefits. Each commodity trade flow must be considered individually.

Britain and our European partners have a moral duty:

• to cease over-producing and dumping products like sugar on the world market
• to give greater priority to the needs of agriculture in developing countries in determining our own agricultural policies.

CHAPTER SIX

Wildlife and Landscape

Wildlife and Landscape

THE DESTRUCTION of the British countryside has been a continual process, spread across several centuries, but the rate at which animals and plants have disappeared has speeded up dramatically over the last forty years, largely as a result of the agricultural and forestry practices which we described in the last chapter. Many species once common are now so rare that they can only be found in nature reserves, and modern farming has created a landscape which is often bleak and monotonous.

In the early years of the eighteenth century Daniel Defoe went on *A Tour Through The Whole Island of Great Britain*. He was neither knowledgeable about wildlife nor particularly interested in it, but he gives us a good idea how much richer the countryside was then. While travelling through Dorset, Defoe notes how young decoy ducks had to be protected from "polecats, kites, and such like"; and he tells of how he found "a monstrous eagle" caught in a trap. The eagle would have been on migration, but polecats and kites were then widespread throughout the country. Now they are confined to a few isolated areas in the uplands. A little later Defoe visited the Fens, where he saw "an infinite number of wild fowl, such as duck and mallard, teal and wigeon, brand geese, wild geese etc, and for the taking of the first four kinds, here are great number of decoys or duckoys, call them which you please, from all which the vast number of fowls they take are sent up to London; the quantity indeed is incredible, and the accounts which the country people give of the numbers they sometimes take, are such, that one scarce dare to report it from them". Nature in such profusion was commonplace then, as it still was a century later when Cobbett went on his *Rural Rides*. He once saw a flock of ten thousand goldfinches near the village of Ocksey. Nowadays a flock of one hundred would be exceptional.

Today it is possible to travel many miles without seeing more than two or three agricultural crops. In Defoe's day the agricultural landscape was much more varied. Hops were found not just in Kent, but in Suffolk, Essex and half a dozen other counties. Flax and hemp were grown on smallholdings from Dorset north to the East Riding of Yorkshire. Liquorice was cultivated in Nottinghamshire and Yorkshire, nightshade in Somerset, camomile in Derbyshire, canary seed in Kent and caraway in Essex. And crops which most people wouldn't recognise today—woad, madder, cole-seed, savory, teasel and saffron—were grown right up to the end of the eighteenth century. Even the crops themselves contained greater variety: the agricultural historian R.E. Prothero reports that two hundred varieties of apple could be found in a single orchard.

There was much to deplore in the countryside of the early nineteenth century. Cobbett found many labourers living in misery, and he railed against the game laws, "which put into the gaols a full third part of the prisoners". Any animals or birds which threatened the harvest of pheasant and partridge were trapped, shot and poisoned, and our birds of prey have never recovered from the slaughter of those days. But farming practices, right up to the Second World War, remained relatively benign. Such a scene as Shelley described in *The Question*—pied windflowers, violets, oxlips and daisies in a meadow; eglantine, cowbind, wild rose and ivy serpentine in a hedge; flag-flowers, water lilies and bulrush in a stream—was familiar to anyone who walked in the countryside half a century ago. It certainly is not today. The countryside of a little while ago not only looked very different, but smelt and sounded different too. Fifty years ago you would have heard stone-curlew on the heaths outside Nottingham, corncrake in the hay-meadows round Sheffield and snipe over the marshy meadows of Brecon. Stone-curlew have virtually disappeared, corncrake are now found only in the Scottish isles and snipe in lowland England and Wales have been reduced from twenty thousand breeding pairs to about two thousand over the last fifteen years. Over much of lowland England the only bird you will hear at night is the tawny owl. Were things as they should be you would hear nightingale, nightjar and barn owl.

Much of the countryside might appear to the casual visitor to be in good heart. However, as we will show in our portrait of the mid-Welsh hills, looks can be deceptive. And frequently we simply do not know what we are missing. The sterilising effects of agricultural practices can best be gauged when an arable field adjoins a block of unreclaimed land. We visited just such an area on the north Norfolk coast, a little way to the west of Hunstanton. It was early July and a sixty-acre field of wheat was beginning to turn a dull beige. The only plants growing here, apart from the wheat, were sterile brome and wild oats, two weeds which the farmer could well have done without. There were no birds nesting in the field, nor any hares or partridge feeding. Nor were there any butterflies or insects. In a month's time the wheat would be combined, the straw burnt and the soil ploughed in preparation for autumn sowing. And so the cycle would repeat itself, year after year.

Ten years ago this area was like the one hundred and eighty acres of grazing marsh which lay beside it. The local naturalists' trust and the landowner had built some small hides on the edge of the marshes. From one we watched a pair of avocets shepherding their young round a small water-filled scrape. Occasionally one of the adults would take flight and wheel, calling musically overhead. Snipe, lapwing, redshank and shelduck was also nesting on the marsh and as we walked across it, past a herd of suckler beef, which were spending the summer fattening up here, we saw and heard skylark, meadow pipit and yellow wagtail, and we put to flight gadwall, teal and shoveller. A marsh harrier slowly flapped its way over the rhines and ditches, in which bred reed and sedge warbler, coot and moorhen. A heron stalked around the edge of a pond in search of newts and frogs, and in a pool near the sand dunes there was a small colony of natterjack toad, Britain's rarest amphibian. All this we saw during an hour's walk. There was much else besides which we didn't see: over one hundred and sixty species of bird have been recorded on the marsh. Floristically the marshes were superb. Half was a sea of yellow buttercups, and in places it was difficult to put a foot down without squashing purple marsh-orchid. Such marshes as these are always changing. In the autumn many of the breeding birds head south, and in their place come great flocks of wintering wildfowl. By November these marshes support over one thousand brent geese, two hundred golden plover, six hundred wigeon, and smaller flocks of lapwing and curlew.

The marshes and the cornfield were separated by a ditch no more than three feet wide, but wildlife does not always respect such boundaries. Whenever birds or animals try to penetrate the 'green desert', conflicts arise with the farmer. Geese are seen as a pest as soon as they stray onto a cornfield, and bird-scarers, which contribute nothing to the peace and quiet of the countryside, are used to drive them off. In the south-east of England, where winter cereals are grown close to the coast, farmers have demanded licences to shoot brent geese which, they maintain, damage their crops. Many other animals and birds find themselves under attack for similar reasons. Yet they are often sentenced to death on the flimsiest of evidence. There is little or no serious scientific work to suggest that brent geese do any significant damage to cereal crops. And allegations that foxes increase lamb mortality are, as we have seen, unsubstantiated by scientific studies: their persecution stems largely from prejudice.

We have said enough in preceding chapters about the scale of wildlife destruction to preclude us from enumerating the losses. However, it is worth looking briefly at why much of the destruction makes little economic sense. Recent studies by the economist J.K. Bowers have highlighted the absurdities of many MAFF-sponsored schemes. He looked at eight cases which had been brought before the Nature Conservancy Council. In each case farmers were applying, as was their right under the 1981 Wildlife and Countryside Act, to be compensated for not developing land of high conservation value. In return for not destroying a particular habitat, a farmer can claim compensation calculated on the basis of profits forgone. But, as Bowers points out, "in compensating the farmer, the NCC is compensating him for a loss of subsidy that he would have received as a consequence of the putative investment. . . A substantial amount of these payments amounts to no more than a transfer of responsibility for paying subsidy from consumers or the central agencies of the CAP to the NCC. . . There is a double irony here: the high level of agricultural support places threats on the environment by making profitable agricultural improvement which otherwise would not be so. Simultaneously it raises the budgetary cost of protecting the environment."

Of the eight cases which Bowers looked at, five investments would not have been profitable in the absence of the support system. "Thus, far from being expensive, conservation is actually saving resources, preventing investment which is properly unprofitable." The Think Tank paper on 'Reducing Agricultural Subsidies' also pointed to the anomalies of the compensation system: "At present 80 per cent of the compensation paid . . . reflects subsidy forgone. In effect, farmers are being subsidised for not being subsidised. This element should be eliminated from compensation payments made under the [Wildlife and Countryside] Act." One is reminded of the farmer who was being subsidised to do nothing in Joseph Heller's *Catch 22*: "His speciality was alfalfa, and he made a good thing out of not growing any. The government paid him well for every bushel of alfalfa he did not grow. The more alfalfa he did not grow, the more money the government gave him, and he spent every penny he didn't earn on new land to increase the amount of alfalfa he did not produce. . . . He invested in land wisely and soon was not growing more alfalfa than any other man in the country."

A study undertaken by the British Association of Nature Conservationists indicated the enormity of the bill which may face the NCC if it is to carry out its statutory duties, which include protecting Britain's sites of special scientific interest (SSSIs). It could come to £42.8 million a year. At 1983 prices the cost of protecting six thousand eight hundred hectares of the Somerset Levels from conversion to cereals that nobody wants is likely to be £27 million over twenty years. And that for protecting just one wood, the two hundred and twenty hectare Boulsbury Wood in Dorset, will be around a third of a million pounds by the end of this century. In 1984 the NCC had just £1.6 million available for the funding of such management agreements.

In 1984 William Waldegrave, the environment minister, described the system of agricultural subsidies as "the engine of destruction", and both the House of Commons Environment Committee in 1983 and the House of Lords Committee on the European Communities in 1984 berated MAFF for being backward-looking and unresponsive to conservation needs. Over the past few years, some attempt has been made by MAFF to improve its public image, and its advisory service has begun to show some interest in advising farmers about conservation. However, a document produced for its officers, 'ADAS [Agricultural Development Advisory Service] Advice on Conservation', shows that conservation is seen as little more than a cosmetic enterprise, and it contains remarkable statements such as "Work...has shown that although improvement of hill land affects bird populations, the effects are not necessarily detrimental and may favour desirable species".

POLICIES FOR NATURE AND LANDSCAPE CONSERVATION

The reforms which we put forward in the previous chapters will do much for conservation. Stricter controls over the use of agro-chemicals will bring about a considerable improvement in the quality of fresh water, thus paving the way for the re-invasion by otters, fish and insects of rivers and lakes which have been reduced to lifelessness by chemical pollution. And controls over the quantities and types of pesticides used will benefit invertebrates and the birds and mammals which prey on them. Reductions in agricultural price support and the abolition of export subsidies will cause some land which has recently been taken into arable production to revert to pasture, and a less intensive, smaller-scale agriculture will do much to enhance the landscape.

We haven't yet referred in any detail to a scourge of our hills that is just as destructive as the most intensive agriculture—taxation forestry. An extremely favourable tax regime has led to a boom in the coniferous afforestation of relatively cheap hill land. The tax concessions and Forestry Commission grants only encourage the planting of non-native conifers. Mounting opposition to the spread of blanket conifers in England and Wales has driven the private forestry companies and their rich clients to Scotland, where almost all new planting now takes place on some of our wildest countryside, rich in moorland birdlife.

The forestry companies make most of their profit from carrying out new planting, so taxation forestry has an insatiable appetite for potentially plantable land. But this money is being spent to benefit a few rich people, destroying wildlife and traditional upland farms in the process. As we discuss later in relation to Central Wales, conifer plantations not only destroy the moors forever, with deep drains and a dark canopy of acid pine needles. These new forests trap acidity from the atmosphere, and the spate floods caused by their new drainage systems pollute water courses, killing fish and other wildlife.

Softwood can be grown cheaper elsewhere, so the industry can only hope to be economic if the public pay up. And as forestry like agriculture, becomes more and more capital- and chemical-intensive, the total number of jobs provided by the industry falls as fast as new land is consumed. This absurdly selfish and short-sighted destruction must end.

We advocate the dismemberment of the Forestry Commission and the abolition of all forms of grant-aid and tax-relief for coniferous afforestation. This will also help to bring back wildlife to areas where spruce and lodgepole pine have excluded it, and an emphasis on replanting with broad-leaved trees will undoubtedly add to the beauty of the countryside. The Forestry Commission's regulatory functions would be taken on by a central government environmental agency, and its forest estates handed over to the county councils. However, the shift towards more benign agricultural and woodland systems, brought about by economic and other reforms, must be augmented by measures which will reward landowners and tenants for fulfilling conservation objectives and which will prevent any further destruction of wildlife habitat.

Obviously, the farmer whose land we looked at on the Norfolk coast could make greater profits by growing wheat than by retaining marshland and grazing suckler beef. The profits on cereals will be substantially less once price support is reduced, but we cannot expect farmers to pursue land-use policies which help conserve wildlife and landscape if, by so doing, they have to deprive themselves of a livelihood.

In some areas, particularly in the lowlands, the production of food will remain the main imperative of farming, and the maintenance of reasonably high levels of fertility will continue to demand substantial inputs, albeit less than today, of artificial fertiliser. As fertile, high-production ecosystems are invariably poor in species, farming and conservation objectives on the same plot of land will be fundamentally irreconcilable. When a farmer fertilises a species-rich meadow its characteristic plants and animals are inevitably destroyed. Environmental damage is intrinsic, not incidental, to chemical farming. However, even in the most intensively farmed areas we can expect to see greater restrictions on the use of chemicals, and we can bring an immediate halt to any further intensification or reclamation. Over much of the rest of the countryside conservation will be the highest priority. In the words of the Think Tank on 'Reducing Agricultural Subsidies', "We believe that in years to come, the best argument for subsidy to the farm industry will be to help conserve the countryside". The corncrake will return to most counties in England, kite will be seen from the tubes in London's suburbia, buzzard will nest in Cambridgeshire and Essex, and before the end of the century it will be difficult to walk anywhere in the countryside at night without hearing nightingales and nightjar.

PLANNING CONTROLS

Agricultural and forestry operations have never been subject to planning controls. It is time they were. Any landowner who wishes to change or remove natural features should have to apply for permission to do so from the county or regional councils. The following activities would all have to be sanctioned by planning authorities: land-drainage; the removal of trees, hedges or woodlands; the conversion of deciduous woodland to other uses; the ploughing of moorland, marshland or heath; and the use of agro-chemicals on land which had hitherto been untreated by artificial fertilisers or pesticides.

Sanctions likewise would give the local community a say about what is done to the land, and decisions on planning applications would be taken by elected representatives. It may be argued—and invariably it is by the agricultural industry—that planning controls would be unwieldy and over-bureaucratic. There is no reason why they should be.

Any sensitive policy for preserving the countryside requires a detailed knowledge of its features. Yet it is over nine centuries since this country carried out a thorough survey of who owns what land and what is in it. The registers of land ownership (except in Scotland) are neither complete nor public. What we need is a new register. Its purpose would be to log the details of every holding. It is the sort of initiative which could be capably undertaken at the parish level. Each tenant or owner would have a farm map containing the following information: land taken up by annual crops, by permanent pasture, by woodland and scrub, ponds and streams, heath and down and so on. Features of special conservation interest should be marked with an indication of their size, age and importance. Copies of the map would be lodged with the council, and the maps would enable the councils to deliberate swiftly on applications for grant-aid and planning permission.

LAND MANAGEMENT PAYMENTS

Land Management Payments (LMPs) would provide a new source of income for landowners who were prepared to sign simple agreements about conservation with the county/regional councils. The agreements would outline management priorities, and the emphasis would be on projects which require inputs of labour rather than capital. For example, if we wish to conserve the hay meadows of the Yorkshire Dales, we must ensure that farmers go on making hay in the traditional way; similarly, if the chalk grasslands of the Kentish Downs are to be maintained, they must be grazed by sheep. Landowners might be given LMPs to help them to establish a coppicing regime in their woodlands; they might claim grants for the upkeep of dry stone walls and other field boundaries or for creating new rights of way or footpaths; and they could, through such a system of compensation, be encouraged to graze beef on marshland which otherwise they might feel inclined to turn into arable prairie.

LMPs would be particularly important for smaller farmers and those on poor land. Payments could be made on a per hectare basis, adjusted according to the nature of the land and the type of the agreement. The scheme would be more comprehensive than ESAs or the Countryside Commission's earlier experimental projects in Halvergate Marshes and the Peak District National Park, where farmers are being encouraged to maintain the traditional landscape. There would be a ceiling on the size of LMP available to each farmer, and payments would be more generous for smallholders and those whose operations required the retention of labour on the land. Cries of 'too expensive!' will come from those opposed. Not true. If one assumes an average payment of £100 a hectare, it would be possible to cover about a third of the entire agricultural area for £700 million a year. This sounds a huge sum, but it should be seen in the context of present agricultural spending: in 1982/3 public expenditure under CAP and on grants and subsidies came to £1,333 million in the UK. As we pointed out in the last chapter, we shall be making considerable savings by reducing price support, altering hill livestock compensatory allowances and doing away with grants for farm roads, land-drainage and so forth.

NATIONAL NATURE RESERVES, VILLAGE NATURE RESERVES AND THE LAND BANK

The United Kingdom has some two hundred and twenty-four national nature reserves (NNRs) which are owned, held by agreement or leased by the NCC. These cover about one hundred and sixty thousand hectares, and they range from small fields and woods to whole mountainsides. Land management within the reserves is dictated entirely by conservation considerations. In addition, there are nearly five thousand SSSIs, covering over one and a half million hectares, where there is a presumption against exploitation inimical to conservation. However, by the early 1980s SSSIs were being damaged or destroyed at the rate of 12 per cent a year. Under our reforms all these sites would be safeguarded, and owners and tenants of SSSIs would be eligible for LMPs. The RSPB owns over eighty reserves, which cover nearly forty thousand hectares, and the county naturalists' trusts manage approximately one thousand three hundred reserves which encompass one hundred and forty-five thousand hectares of land. Local authorities are empowered to create local nature reserves, but they have been notably laggard in doing so. There are less than a hundred, and their average size is a mere one hundred and twenty-seven hectares. In short, the percentage of land in Britain whose primary purpose is nature conservation is tiny.

The Land Bank, whose functions we discussed in Chapter Five, will increase the amount of protected land four- or five-fold, and even in parts of the Land Bank where forestry and recreation are seen as the main priorities, conservation interests will be well served. For example, the planting of sixteen thousand hectares or more of deciduous woodland in Sherwood Forest (discussed in the final chapter) will provide not only timber and jobs but a vast habitat in which pine marten, wild boar, red deer, buzzard and barn owl will flourish alongside more common species like nuthatch, tree-creeper, nightingale, badger and fox.

We are particularly keen that parishes, or their equivalent, should establish their own village nature reserves. These might cover just a hectare or so, or they might be of a size comparable to local naturalists' trust nature reserves (which are an average twelve hectares each). How such patches of land are managed would be entirely the responsibility of the local communities, although they could seek advice from the NCC or other expert organisations. Some parishes might wish to establish recreation facilities. In some parts of the country parishes have already created their own reserves. For example, below the mining village of Blidworth in Nottinghamshire, there is a two-acre patch of grass and scrub. It was bought from a local farmer by the parish council, and the county council gave a grant which was used to buy picnic tables and plant trees. It is a delightful spot, much used by the villagers, and just the sort of thing we would like to see right across the country. As one of the council officers put it: "Every village should have one". If the parish council isn't interested in setting up its own reserve, then voluntary bodies should be encouraged to do so.

Nature should be made more available, and with a little effort it could be. Many nature reserves, especially those owned by the RSPB, have hides which enable the visitor to see birds at close quarters. These give great pleasure to many people and help them to observe wildlife which they might otherwise not get close to. There is no reason why hides should be restricted to nature reserves. The landowner whose Norfolk marshes we visited had built a hide on the edge of his marshland, to which it was just a short walk from the nearest village. It overlooked a large pond, and a book in which locals and visitors wrote down their observations told of what could be seen here. Some entries just commented on the weather; others described harriers feeding, the arrival of winter migrants, and birds nesting round the edge of the pond. Facilities like these are cheap to build and add immeasurably to the enjoyment of many people, whether they are expert naturalists or casual walkers.

HUNTING, SHOOTING AND KILLING

Our attitudes towards what it is reasonable to kill, and what it is not, are remarkably inconsistent. The British have a passion for large, furry creatures and for small birds. Implicit in the question, "Who killed cock robin?", is a crime committed. We are outraged by the trappers of Italy who kill nightingales and willow warblers, and by Canadians who kill baby seals, but what greater claim to life do these creatures have than the fox, the stoat, the pigeon, the grouse and the pheasant, which are variously considered either vermin or fair game? The answer is none.

In putting forward suggestions about what we should and should not be allowed to kill, we touch on a very difficult area, and for a number of reasons. First, however much one abhors the taking of life, there is no doubt that for some wildlife some form of control is necessary. Even the vegan must recognise that the food on his or her plate comes from fields where eelworms, leather-jackets and weavils have been eliminated. And second, and perhaps more importantly, it is part of the liberal creed that one cannot legislate to make people 'good'. However, much of what happens in blood sports is contrary to the interests of not only the quarry, but of its predators, which are persecuted as 'vermin', and of the many people who find such sports deeply offensive and upsetting. Shooting and hunting lock up the land and make it inaccessible. There are large tracts of moorland from which the public is excluded for the sake of grouse-shooting and deer stalking. To give but one example, the farms on the twenty three thousand six hundred and forty acre Killilan estate in south-west Ross are now unworked, largely because the previous owners, the Wills tobacco family, were more interested in stalking deer than keeping people on the land.

At present, legislation exists to protect some species of mammal, bird, reptile, amphibian and fish, and these are listed in the relevant schedule of the 1987 Wildlife and Countryside Act. We believe that the presumption in law should be that all species of mammal and bird be protected, with certain exceptions. The exceptions should include three 'pests' which can cause economic damage and which are common: the brown rat, the house mouse and the rabbit. The killing of foxes, stoats, weasels, magpies, jays, birds of prey and all other creatures commonly regarded as vermin by shooting interests should be banned. However, farmers and landowners should be able to apply for permission to kill species other than the rabbit, rat and mouse if they believe they are causing problems. If they prove that damage of a serious nature is being done, then they could be given a limited pest-control licence. There are some animals which, both for their own sake and that of others, must periodically be culled. This is particularly true for species which are no longer preyed upon by their natural predator and which could expand over most of the countryside, finding food on all agricultural land. Now that the wolf has gone from this country, deer populations must be kept to a level where they do not do too much damage to forests and crops.

CHAPTER SEVEN

The Countryside
We Want

The Countryside We Want

THOSE WHO bemoan the changes in the countryside have frequently failed to suggest, except in the haziest of terms, what they would like to see happen. It is all very well to say that we want a countryside with more wildlife, less pollution, greater opportunities for work and so forth, but how can we get it? And what exactly will it feel and look like? In this chapter we take three areas in England and Wales and for each we describe how the countryside once was, how it is now, and how it could be in the future.

NORTH KENT

The naturalist who led us round the hills behind Lane End village had spent his childhood here in the 1950s. He hadn't been back since. As a child he could set out from his home below Darenth Park Mental Hospital and spend a day wandering through rich deciduous woodland and across chalk downland without ever crossing a major road. Dartford and London lay over the hills to the north-west, but this little valley, through which runs the River Darent, where he would catch crayfish and observe fat cattle feeding in lush meadows, was thoroughly rural: "I used to think I lived in deep countryside," he said. Today, even in the middle of Darenth Wood, you cannot escape the noise of motor traffic. The A2 has chopped the wood in half, and a little to the west of Lane End it links in to the M25.

The fields below Darenth Park used to be grazed by the hospital's herd of Ayrshire cows. Now they are down to barley, as are the fields on the other side of a chestnut-lined road which heads up the hill. "I used to come up here in the evenings," said our guide as we tramped onto a patch of downland near the hilltop. "It was thick with rabbits." That was before myxomatosis wiped out most of them. There isn't much chalk downland left in Kent now, and much of what remains is reverting to scrub as there are neither the sheep nor rabbits to graze it. While the lower slopes have been ploughed out and put down to cereals, the steeper ones have been abandoned.

This little remnant was still very colourful. Purple pyramid orchids grew in profusion, and there were yellow splashes of colour from mouse-eared hawkweed and bird's-foot trefoil. The white flowers of ox-eye daisy nodded in the breeze, and viper's bugloss and purging flax added a strong blue and pale violet to the rich turf. But ash and hawthorn have already reclaimed much of the hillside and unless the area is grazed or burnt the chalk downland flowers will disappear before the end of the century.

Crossing the A2 into the northern half of the wood was a major operation—there is only one foot-bridge along the three-mile stretch between Swanscombe Park and the M25 junction—but it was well worth the trouble. It is a lovely wood, dominated by oak and birch, though in places given over to ash and sweet chestnut, both of which used to be coppiced. Where the soil is acid there are patches of heather and bracken. Elsewhere there is a thick carpet of dog's mercury beneath a shrub layer of hazel, holly and ash. There are even a few wild service-trees. Their fruit, known as chequers, used to be made into beer: hence the many Chequers Inns in this part of Kent. The naturalist was pleasantly surprised by the woodland: "It's hardly changed at all," he said, "apart from the roads." When he was young the Dover traffic had to go along Watling Street. The A2 has obliterated one footpath and crossed others, and signs tacked onto trees are evidently meant to frighten people off. 'Shooting with Silenced Rifle,' said one; 'Beware Adders,' read another.

The countryside east of Dartford has become noisier in one way, quieter in another. The roads have put paid to rural tranquillity, but the fields and woods are almost devoid of working people. Twenty years ago you would have seen psychiatric patients out in the fields herding their cows and shepherds looking after their sheep. In the woods you would have found coppicers chopping down trees and preparing wood for fence stakes and sheep hurdles. But Darenth Park Hospital is about to close and dairy herding as a form of therapy went out of fashion years ago. Coppicing has ceased too and the farmers have moved out of stock-rearing into arable cropping, which demands plenty of chemicals but little labour. There are still gypsies in the woods, though they have now been settled in small prefabricated houses on the edge of the A2.

In short, the landscape is lifeless, and the saddest symbol of its present state is another hospital just to the north of Lane End. It was closed down four years ago, and its playing fields and formal gardens are gradually returning to waste. Ornamental roses still poke out among the nettles, but the flights of steps which climb up the hillside and the footpaths in the nearby parkland are overgrown and in places almost impassable. 'Keep Out' signs ring the area. A lone security guard sat in a wheelchair listening to Radio 1 when we arrived. He was understandably nervous. Arsonists had set fire to one building the previous night, and each week vandals do what nature would, given slightly longer.

Yet the changes which have occurred in this valley over the last twenty years are nothing to what has happened on the other side of Watling Street. "When I was a boy," recalled the naturalist as we looked east from the B259, "this was farmland". Now there is a very large hole, covering about eighty acres to a depth of some one hundred feet below the road. It is one of the great chalk pits in this part of Kent. The excavations have gone well below the water table in some places, and already birch and hawthorn have begun to recolonise bare worked-out surfaces. There have always been chalk pits round here, for example, there was one just off the main road from Dartford to Lane End. It was probably about five acres, but it has been filled in and grassed over.

There is little point in mourning the changes which have already happened here. Given the power of the road transport lobby, it was inevitable that a motorway would be built to link London to Dover, and the building boom since the last war meant that chalk had to come from somewhere. It is sad that the Dartford warbler, which appears on the crest of Dartford hospitals and was once so common on the heaths, is now a rarity seldom seen outside Dorset and Hampshire, and it is equally sad that a countryside once full of people working and tending stock is now producing either unwanted corn or being left to revert to scrub. The lower reaches of the Darent Valley have lost their rurality and acquired the unkempt and rubbish-tipped appearance typical of the modern urban fringe. What matters is that we should make the best of what remains. First, however, let us imagine the worst that might happen here.

There are huge deposits of chalk beneath the mental hospital, and the triangle between Watling Street, the A2 and the road linking the two to the west of the hospital could profitably be dug out. Watling Street would become like many other roads in this area: a thin ribbon lined by a single row of houses whose gardens end abruptly on the cliff tops of the chalk pits. With this would come more noise, more heavy traffic and more dust.

The house builders must already have their eyes on the abandoned hospital beside Lane End. Its grounds are spacious and it would be an ideal setting for a commuter development. Fifty or so up-market mock-Georgian houses would fit in just nicely. The woodland round the hospital grounds could be pared away or modified into parkland and the few farmers who remain in the valley, tired of vandalism and depressed by the falling profitability of growing cereals, could easily be persuaded to part with their land. Barley fields would go under more housing and the few patches of chalk grassland and heath would either revert to scrub or be landscaped to give the newcomers somewhere to walk on summer evenings.

This, of course, is a very simplistic projection. Nevertheless, it is quite possible that by the year 2000 the village of Lane End could lie at the heart of a medium-sized new town, bordered by the existing motorways and freshly dug chalk pits. It would then become part of Dartford, which means another suburb of London. Today you can walk from St Paul's Cathedral to Darenth Park Hospital without ever being clear of housing and industrial development. You cannot walk from Dartford to Lane End without passing through a field: it is still countryside—just.

Now let us look at how fine a valley this could become. The motorways are a *fait accompli*, so we must accept them; and the hospitals are destined to go, so that too we must accept.

The land which is presently farmed, or was until recently, should continue to be farmed, though very differently. The soils here are poor, and it has only been the exceptional incentives given to cereal production that have brought all the valley-bottom fields into barley. Having got rid of their stock, the farmers have allowed the unploughable slopes of grassland to revert to scrub. We want to retain all this herb-rich habitat, both here and where it is found in the rest of the country.

Indeed from a conservation point of view this is a high priority. We must either burn it regularly, as happens on many nature reserves, or it must be grazed. We favour the latter course. Taking that course opens a pastoral vision of immense appeal. Small flocks of Downs-bred sheep could be hefted from one plot of grassland to another. This would maintain floristic richness and provide work. In some cases the shepherds might also have fields in the valley bottoms, where they could grow vegetables and perhaps keep a few cows or pigs. Some of the fields could be given over to hay or turnips. The hay would be used as winter feed, and in the winter months the sheep could eat the turnips off the fields. Such a system would involve a reversion to old-fashioned methods of crop rotation, thus reducing the need for artificial fertilisers or pesticides. Ideally, this land would come into public ownership and the smallholders and shepherds would become tenants of the county council. Switching from the present system of cereal cropping to stock-rearing smallholdings would save public money, even though the small-holders would require—initially, at least—an income supplement to help them survive.

Darenth Wood, which is already a valuable wildlife site, could be put to more adventurous use. A coppicing regime could be re-established for the sweet chestnut and the ash, and if the same were to happen in other Kent woodlands, which have been allowed to revert to high forest, there is no reason why an industry for long in decline should not thrive again. The county council would be the ideal body to co-ordinate such a scheme. The wood could also be of great value for recreation. There is already a scrambling pit on its east side. Signs like 'Beware Adders' and 'Do Not Trespass' would all come down and people would be free to wander where they chose, either on footpaths or off.

There are two possibilities for the abandoned hospital and its grounds by Lane End. We certainly wouldn't be averse to some housing development. What we object to is the creation of affluent enclaves where the houses are priced well beyond the means of those in our cities who have most need of decent housing. Were any building to take place here we would like it to be done by the local authority and rented to local people. Alternatively, the grounds, together with the woods, would make an ideal country park and the area could simply be managed for 'informal recreation'.

Worked-out chalk pits are generally put to one of two uses. They are either flooded and turned into boating lakes, of which there is no shortage in the London area, or they are used as municipal rubbish-dumps. It is time to be more imaginative. Those near Dartford could be left to nature and, with a little management turned into oak-forest.

THE MID-WELSH HILLS

"Nowhere is safe in mid-Wales," said our guide. "What the farmers can't plough up and reseed, the foresters cover with Sitka spruce." Forty years ago the hills to the north and west of Llanwrtyd Wells were part of a traditional upland landscape. The steeper slopes of the Irfon and Towy valleys were clothed in oak-forest, and the valley bottoms contained a patchwork of marshland and hay meadow. Sheep passed the summer months on the hills and came down to the valleys in the winter. It was archetypal dog-and-stick country. It has changed beyond all recognition, with MAFF and the Forestry Commission zealously encouraging landowners to 'improve' their land.

A farm near Beulah typifies what has happened. The in-bye land which runs either side of a stream is a livid lime-green—'Fison's green'. EEC grants have been used to drain, plough and reseed damp and floristically rich meadows. These hedged-in fields used to support breeding lapwing, snipe and curlew, all of which have gone. This farmer has kept his hedges, but here, as over much of Radnor and

Brecon, they have been fenced in. Such is the intensity of grazing that hedges, whose purpose is to control stock movement, must be protected from the sheep, which otherwise would eat them out.

Over the last twenty years, ninety per cent of the hay meadows and unimproved pastures in mid-Wales have disappeared. In 1982 Welsh farmers in the Less Favoured Areas (which, roughly speaking, encompass all land eight hundred feet or more above sea level) received £3.4 million from the EEC and central government for 'grassland improvement'. The effect, however, is often temporary, and frequently one comes across reclaimed grassland which is reverting to rough pasture. One field we came across further up the valley from Beulah looked as though it had been used for tank training. It was full of deep ruts and unfinished furrows. All attempts at drainage have failed.

The farm near Beulah has two miles of oak-wood, some hundred yards deep, ribboning round the steep hillside. It has one hundred and twenty species of higher plant. And among the breeding birds are sparrow hawk, buzzard, pied flycatcher and green and lesser-spotted woodpeckers. All in all it is rather special. Yet the farmer has already felled a good deal of it. The ruse is a simple one. You apply for a tree-felling licence from the Forestry Commission and agree to replant with broad-leaved trees. After five years you can grub out the saplings, plough it up and reseed with rye grass. As it happens, over ninety per cent of the oak-woods in mid-Wales are so heavily grazed that there is no regeneration, so unless they are fenced against stock they will eventually disappear. We were told of one farmer who had lopped off the lower branches of all his oak trees, then rotavated the forest floor and reseeded it.

From a distance these woodlands appear very lovely. It is only when you get close that you realise something is wrong. They are like the manicured parks of our cities, with an even canopy of mature trees standing over a close-cropped turf.

Were these healthy forests with a future there would be a thick understorey of bramble and scrub along with new oak saplings.

Twenty years ago the hilltops round here would have been clothed with heather and bilberry. Today many of them too are Fison's green. Yet again, sheep and the EEC are responsible. In Britain's LFAs farmers can claim hill livestock compensatory allowances. In 1986 the estimated bill for sheep came to £21.1 million, and the figure for 1987 will be similar. There is a maximum payment per hectare, but the number of eligible sheep is so high that over-grazing is inevitable.

A decade ago farmers were required to register their common land grazing rights. In some cases, where the commons were small and the claimants many, farmers registered rights which, were they to excercise them simultaneously, would require sheep to be stacked two or three deep just to fit them on the common. Many of the commons of mid-Wales have been overgrazed and heather is becoming a rarity.

The road building which swathed the countryside south of Dartford with concrete seems almost restrained compared to that which is going on in rural Wales. In 1982 Welsh farmers in LFAs received £2.8 million in grants towards building farm roads. In some instances the building of roads may be justified; often it is not. MAFF has adopted the attitude that if a farmer is prepared to put up his share towards costs then he can build as many roads as he wishes. We saw one road which went nowhere, and it was impossible to divine what use it could have been to the farmer. Often roads have been used as an excuse to chop down woods.

The greatest changes, however, have come through coniferous afforestation. There is an almost continuous band of Sitka spruce stretching from Strata Florida on the River Teifi twenty miles south to Llandovery. In places it is eight miles wide. Many thousands of acres of oak woods and rough grazing, which once supported a wealth of wildlife, are now a uniform and relatively lifeless glaucous green. Such has been the impact of forestry here that even the Secretary of State for Wales felt some restraint was necessary two years ago. He turned down a proposal by the Economic Forestry Group to afforest six hundred acres of the Nant-y-Brain Common, which was the last remaining block of open land between Llanwrtyd Wells and Strata Florida. Had he not done so it would have been possible to walk through a continuous fifteen-mile corridor lined with spruce. Some of the local population are so fed up with the scale of forestry operations that arson has become a major problem, and there are areas in South Wales where the Forestry Commission realises there is no point in planting up any more land. The coniferous forests have done more than spoil the landscape and drive off farmers and wildlife (the sparrow hawk is one of the few species which has benefited): they have compounded the problem of river acidification. Conifers concentrate atmospheric acid and this causes soils to release aluminium salts, which are washed into the rivers in the flash floods which the new forestry encourages. The Irfon, a tributary of the Wye, is now devoid of fish. It used to support a healthy population of dippers, small birds which feed on aquatic insects. There is now only one pair left.

If we wish to apportion blame for what has happened in mid-Wales, then to whom should we direct it? Quite clearly to MAFF and the Forestry Commission. Both have been supremely effective in inducing farmers and landowners to abandon traditional forms of low-input farming. "If a farmer has an old meadow round here," said our guide, "he is considered drunk or insane. No way will an efficient farmer keep one." And while MAFF has provided the money to upgrade the pastures, the chemical companies have taken full advantage. "They're like drug peddlars round here," we were told. "They come with their fertilisers, their pesticides and their seed mixes, and they've made huge profits." So even in this remote corner of Wales, farmers have been lured onto the chemical treadmill which is all too familiar to the arable farmers of lowland Britain.

The irony is that the EEC's Less Favoured Areas directive was not meant to promote the destructive forms of farming typical now in Radnor. As Peter Walker, a former Minister of Agriculture, once said: "The principal objective of the Directive is not to encourage production, but to compensate farmers in order to ensure the continuation of farming." Yet production has rocketed (the number of breeding ewes in the UK rose by a further 1.4 per cent in the year ending June 1985, an increase of two hundred and forty thousand animals), while the numbers working in the uplands have steadily declined. Two-thirds of full-time jobs were lost from Dartmoor and Exmoor between 1952 and 1972: seventy-nine per cent of full-time jobs disappeared in Snowdonia between 1965 and 1973. "The image of the struggling small farmer is nothing but a myth round here," said one observer. Increasingly, the bigger farmers have been buying out the smaller ones, and 'down country' farms and firms have moved in, ripped out the hedges and created 'prairie hills'. (You can now find areas in Radnor Forest where open moorland over two thousand feet has been converted to rye grass and clover.) Nor has forestry done anything to stem the population decline. In Wales the Forestry Commission employs only one man for every two hundred and ninety acres of forest.

The picture is bleak. Large amounts of public money are being used to keep a declining number of farmers on the hills, which they are being encouraged to destroy in order to get it. There is an atmosphere of bitterness and conflict which is unknown in the lowlands. The Farmers' Union of Wales has made it clear that it will do everything it can to thwart the efforts of the conservation bodies, and if present government apathy about the state of the uplands prevails for another decade, it will doubtless succeed in its objective.

Neither sheep farming nor coniferous forestry would make any economic sense in mid-Wales were it not for the subsidies. Ecologically, when practised on the present scale, they make no sense at all. Our objectives are three-fold. We must ensure that a healthy, viable human community remains. We must protect what remains of the wildlife and bring a great deal back. And we must encourage a form of stewardship which creates a landscape which will attract tourism, the only industry which is capable of bestowing prosperity not just upon the farmers, who are a minority of the local population, but on all who live in the Welsh uplands.

It is vital that all the remaining oak-woods, hay meadows and rough pastures be conserved. Headage payments constitute a form of production payment. They encourage expansion of the sheep flock. They should be abolished. In their place farmers should be given direct income-supplements, which would be calculated individually on the basis of need. The sheep flock, at a rough estimate, should be halved, and maximum stocking densities should be set at between half or a third of the present level laid down in the LFA directives.

There should be a moratorium on the felling of all deciduous woodland. And almost all sheep-grazing within the woods should cease. Grants should be paid to farmers and contractors to fence the woodland. This would be a consid-erable task, and it would require a large workforce. Capital grants for grassland improvement, land drainage and the building of farm roads would be abolished, and there would be a general presumption, which could be legally enforced by the county council, against the ploughing out or 'improve-ment' of all remaining hay meadows and rough pasture.

In a sense all we shall be doing is emphasising the social objectives of the much-misinterpreted LFA directive. We shall be paying farmers to conserve a traditional landscape while enabling them to continue, albeit on a more modest scale, a way of life which is familiar to them. We believe that farmers should receive income supplements if they can show that the profits from their land are too meagre to sustain themselves and their families. Grants should be made available for those who wish to set up tourism or craft enterprises, and MAFF would be empowered to pay farmers to manage their woodlands and meadows in ways which protect their conservation interest.

We do not wish to see any further diminution in the number of farms in mid-Wales. Some farmers, loath to go along with new policies, may decide to sell up, in which case the local authority should have the first option to buy. The authority's main priority, one hopes, would be to establish smallholdings, which it would rent out to those who wished to get on the farming ladder, but who, through lack of capital, have hitherto been unable to do so.

Our attitude towards the Forestry Commission is unequivocal. We wish to see it abolished, along with all special tax concessions to conifer forestry. In this area the Commission's estates should be handed over to county councils. It would then be up to the councils to determine what should be done with the Sitka spruce forests. In time many could be made very attractive and their wildlife interest could be enhanced. Selective felling and the creation of glades would leave a more open landscape, and grants would be made available to restock with hardwood trees. The recreation potential of such forests would be considerable. As far as private forestry interests are concerned, we do not believe any direct intervention is necessary. Very few would plant conifers were it not for the grants and tax incentives made available through the Commission. Once these are abolished we shall see an end to new plantings, and the only way a landowner would be able to make his established forests pay would be by returning them to hardwoods.

Reforms such as these would transform the hills round Llanwrtyd Wells. The great monotonous carpet of spruce would be broken up, the oak-woods would once again develop an understorey, and hills whose vegetation is cropped to a few inches would be recolonised by bilberry and heather. Bird and animal life would undoubtedly benefit. Birds of wet pasture would return to areas from which intensive farming has recently excluded them. And with their return the valleys will once again resound to the drumming of snipe and the cries of the curlew.

The local community would gain as the area became increasingly attractive to holiday-makers. The reforms we advocate would create a whole variety of jobs and help stem depopulation. There would be free public access to all the fields and forests, which there isn't at present, and the countryside would be altogether more lively, with more people working and walking in it.

SHERWOOD FOREST

The Dukeries pub is a large and unprepossessing building, cast in red brick, just down the lane from an abandoned rail station whose four platforms have been taken over by weeds. It was built during Victorian times for the tourists who came to the small and prosperous mining town of Edwinstowe from Nottingham, Newark, Mansfield and Worksop. Some of the visitors would spend a few nights at the pub; many would drop in for refreshment before walking through the town and heading into Birklands, the last surviving fragment of the ancient woodlands which, during Norman times, stretched from the Wirral in Cheshire to the Trent in Nottinghamshire. Sherwood Forest has been in the tourism business for as long, if not longer, than most seaside resorts. Last year over a million visits were made to the country parks at Birklands and Rufford, both of which are run by Nottinghamshire County Council, and as many again to Clumber Park, which is owned by the National Trust.

Sherwood was one of the royal hunting forests established by the Norman kings. It provided timber and food for the local population, and the nobility came here on hunting trips. It is said that Edward I convened a parliament under an oak near Clipstone, but it has been the legend of Robin Hood which has ensured the fame of Sherwood Forest. Reductions in its extent were well under way by the time of King John, and by the thirteenth century it covered a mere one hundred thousand acres, about one-fifth of the county of Nottinghamshire. Sherwood's history as a royal hunting forest came to an end after the reign of Charles I and more woodland was cleared and the land put to agricultural use by the landlords who took it over. The northern half of the forest area has been known as the Dukeries for the past two centuries, as at one time it was owned by four dukes and two lords. The pattern of landownership still reflects this feudalism, though the Rufford and Clumber estates are now country parks, and the Thoresbury estate leases much of its land to the County Council and the Forestry Commission.

What remains north of Edwinstowe gives some idea of the mosaic of oak forest, heathland and scrub which once stretched from Worksop south as far as Nottingham. The woods at Birklands contain some magnificent oaks, a few as old as five hundred years, their hollow bowls so wide that half a dozen people can comfortably stand inside them. Many are in the slow process of dying, with dead trunks hanging like rotten limbs and awaiting a good storm to break them to the ground, where they will gradually be consumed by fungi and insects. Even in medieval times there would have been much open land in Sherwood Forest. Some of it would have been heathland; and some would have been slowly reverting through birch scrub to high forest. The mix of habitats at Birklands still attracts a wealth of wildlife. There are over sixty species of breeding birds, and the diverse insect population has led to it being designated a SSSI. However, the populations of many animals have declined and some species have disappeared. At one time thousands of red deer would have roamed the Forest. Now there are no more than fifty. Swine—the forerunners of the domestic pig—would have foraged in the forest along with wild boar, and pine marten would have preyed on small mammals and birds, while wolf must have competed with royalty for venison.

The changes over the last forty years have been every bit as great as those which occured when the dukes carved out their estates and sunk the first large coal-pits here. But despite the changes it remains a delightful landscape and a lively one. One cannot go for more than a few miles on the drive north from Nottingham to Birklands without catching sight of the winding gear which whirrs above the pits, and villages like Blidworth, Rainworth, Clipstone and Edwinstowe owe their present vitality to the thick seams of coal below the Forest.

We have said enough about coniferous afforestation in mid-Wales to save us from further expressing our views on the subject, except to say that the land north of Rainworth is now carpeted with a two thousand-acre blanket of Corsican pine, and Birklands is hemmed in on three sides by conifers. Of the one hundred and sixty thousand acres which the County Council still designates as Sherwood Forest, approximately half are in forestry. The rest, save for a few small patches of heath, is farmed.

Since 1970 there has been a dramatic increase in arable cropping in Sherwood Forest. The amount of land down to sugar beet has increased by seventy-five per cent, and the number of acres growing rape has risen from less than five to more than one thousand. The potato acreage has gradually risen, though less spectacularly, and cereals have become much more widespread. The area on which wheat is grown has doubled since 1970, and our guide was constantly pointing to fields of corn which just a few years ago had been covered with birch, heather, bilberry and bracken. Not only has the landscape been transformed, but access to it has suffered. These trends have been familiar over much of lowland England. However, the soils here, which are dry, sandy and thin, are unsuited to arable cropping and it has only been the high support prices available for these crops, combined with heavy inputs of fertiliser and irrigation, which have made it worth the farmers' while to reclaim land. The soil is so porous that the irrigation pumps in the beet fields must sometimes continue working even when it is raining hard, as it was on the August day when we visited the forest.

The Bunter sandstone is an important aquifer which provides drinking water for the neighbouring towns. As far back as 1970 the nitrate in Worksop's water exceeded the maximum permissible level laid down by the World Health Organisation. Artificial fertiliser, without which arable cropping would be impractical, is quickly washed through these soils into the ground-water, and there are serious worries about the effects nitrates may have on the health of those who drink polluted water. It is a classic case of unsuitable farming practices being sustained by an economic policy which is formulated without reference to soil chemistry. There is little doubt that if the EEC's guaranteed prices for cereals are reduced over the coming years, which seems highly probable, the farmers in Sherwood Forest, particularly those on the least fertile soils who do not irrigate, will be forced to abandon arable cropping.

Sherwood Forest would be an ideal area for set-aside. At present, farming is sustained in Sherwood Forest at great public cost and to the detriment of the soils, the aquifers and the wildlife. The forest is already of immense importance for tourism and it provides a valuable green lung for those who live in the nearby towns of the east Midlands. Nottinghamshire County Council, which is recognised as one of the more enlightened in its countryside management, already plays an important role in providing tourist facilities in the Forest. It runs adventurous interpretative centres at

Birklands and Rufford, and it subsidises the excellent Sherwood Forester bus service. (Two adults and up to three children can buy a family ranger-ticket which will take them to all the main sites in the forest for just £2 a day). The council spends approximately £2 million a year on environmental improvement schemes, which have benefited many of the mining villages, and over the last ten years the number employed in its countryside division has risen from three people to sixty full-time and eighty part-time workers.

Over much of rural Britain, small towns and villages have been taken over by an affluent commuter population which has moved out from the industrial centres. The indigenous working class who have remained in their villages have found themselves increasingly isolated, and they have been the ones to suffer as public transport and other services have been cut. The towns and villages of Sherwood Forest have yet to experience this rural gentrification, and it is vital that we put into action now policies which will ensure that they don't when the coal begins to run out in twenty or thirty years' time. The miners' strike highlighted the problems which are created when mines are closed in villages and towns where coal has been the mainstay of the economy, and where no alternative work has been provided for those who lose their jobs. Future plans for the Forest should be predicated on the inevitable exhaustion of coal early next century, and they should build on the area's potential for recreation and the production of high quality hardwood products.

This, briefly, is what we would do. We would immediately bring all arable land in the area out of production, and replant with deciduous woodland or allow it to revert to heathland. The coniferous forests could gradually be cropped, and they would be replanted with oak and other hardwoods. Over the next century we could expect to create forty to fifty thousand acres of woodland similar to that which was here in medieval times. Such a woodland would employ hundreds of local people, some as rangers and foresters, others in the manufacturing industry which would process the wood and produce furniture, building timbers or whatever there was a market for. We would expect a substantial amount of money to be spent on promoting tourism and creating holiday villages within the woods. This, too, would provide many new jobs.

The new woodlands and heaths would add enormously to the wildlife of the area. The red deer herd could be increased from its present handful to a thousand or more, and the Forest would become an ideal place to reintroduce the wild boar, which has been absent from Britain for over two hundred years, but which still flourishes in many parts of France without causing problems for agriculture. The ancient practices of free-ranging pigs in oak forests could also be taken up again. Traditional breeds like the Gloucester Old Spot and the Tamworth would not only be beneficial to the woodlands and of interest to the walker, but they could provide the sort of high quality free-range meat for which there is a growing market.

Outside the country parks, public access in Sherwood Forest is very limited. The conversion of heaths to cereal fields has obliterated many paths, often illegally, and some exceptionally lovely landscapes must be viewed from roads rather than walked across. The Repton Lakes on the Wellbeck Estate, for example, are inaccessible. There are no paths along the water's edge, and the beauty of the Great Lake has already been spoilt by the strip of arable farm land which runs along its northern side. Farming practices have locked up the landscape. We would open it up again.

We envisage the day when the visitor to Sherwood Forest, free to go wherever he or she pleases, will have a chance of seeing red deer, wild boar and foraging pigs. Stone curlews will return to the heaths along with nightjar and stonechat, and buzzards, red kite and sparrowhawk will breed in the woodlands. There will also be many more people working in the woods, either in jobs related to the tourist industry or looking after and exploiting the woods.

Today it is difficult to walk anywhere without feeling that we are walking on someone else's land, and that we can only do so because the landowner generously permits. We intend to create a countryside—not just in Sherwood Forest and the mid-Welsh hills but throughout Britain—where we shall not feel indebted to the landowner, whether the owner be a county council, a private individual or the NCC. We shall feel that the countryside is as much ours as anybody else's, and we shall take collective pride in its beauty and richness. We do not see, as part of this countryside, landowners appearing out of hedgebacks to confront us with begging bowls. We wish them prosperity, but their prosperity must not derive from selfish forms of land use which prevent others working and walking in the countryside. It is abundantly clear that unless positive plans are made now for Sherwood Forest, it will be a very sad place in thirty years time. The survival of the communities in Edwinstowe, Rainworth and the other small towns can only be ensured by recreating the woodlands and building up the tourist industry. Much of Britain's agricultural landscape will continue to be farmed, albeit somewhat differently than it is today. But Sherwood is one of the areas which shouldn't be.

Epilogue

As Peter Melchett notes in the foreword to this book, this is a time of confusion for the British countryside. That confusion arises principally because policies which have ruled for decades (for half a century in some important cases) are being unmade. But this is being done piecemeal. New policies, where they are emerging at all, do so *ad hoc* and in response to urgent pressures rather than as the result of careful thought.

Politicians (whether in or out of office) do not have a comprehensive vision of the future countryside. And it is just such a comprehensive vision that we have sought to provide here. Readers do not need to agree with all our propositions to see the benefits of such an approach.

Surely the horrors rural Britain has been made to suffer in recent years are proof enough of what happens when policies are made or maintained to satisfy sectional groups. Forestry to cure the tax headache of the wealthy; planning rules which explode some villages while condemning others to gentrification; farm support engineered by barley barons for barley barons; buses and trains devastated by subservience to the private transport lobbies—these are but few examples.

By the time you read this, ministers and their policies may be different. We hope so. But even if they are, the message of our manifesto will remain valid and useful. Ministers who go their own way and place themselves in hock to special interests, ministries and civil servants who serve the industries they are sponsoring rather than the public, these characterise administrations of every political stripe. They are problems which any government, however radical its motives and universal its platform, must face. We hope that *The Countryside We Want* will help them through the maze. For, at the end of it, beckons the shining vision which William Langland gave to Piers Plowman looking down upon

the countryside from the Malvern Hills on a May morning six
centuries ago:

> A fair field full of folk. . .
> Of all manner of men, the mean and the rich,
> Working and wandering as the world asketh.

GLOSSARY

ADAS	Agricultural Development Advisory Service
BBONT	Berks, Bucks, and Oxon Naturalists' Trust
CAP	Common Agricultural Policy
CLA	Country Landowners' Association
COMA	Committee on Medical Aspects of Food Policy
DoE	Department of the Environment
EEC	European Economic Community
ESA	Environmentally Sensitive Area
HSA	Housing Stress Area
LFA	Less Favoured Area
LMP	Land Management Payment
MAFF	Ministry of Agriculture, Fisheries and Food
MoD	Ministry of Defence
MSC	Manpower Services Commission
NACNE	National Advisory Committee on Nutrition Education
NCC	National Conservancy Council
NNR	National Nature Reserve
NFU	National Farmers' Union
RSPB	Royal Society for the Protection of Birds
SCG	Socialist Countryside Group
SSSI	Site of Special Scientific Interest

ERRATUM

Please note correct title for C.P.R.E.:
Council for the Protection of Rural England